Pitch Like A Pro

Decoding Investor Pitch

Expert tips and insider secrets to elevate your pitch and secure the funding your business deserves.

CA B M AGGARWAL

PITCH LIKE A PRO: Decoding Investor Pitch
Copyright © 2023 B M Aggarwal

Pitch Like A Pro
Decoding Investor Pitch

Pitch like a pro: Expert tips and insider secrets to elevate your pitch and secure the funding your business deserves.

CA B M AGGARWAL

CONTENTS

Dedication

This book is dedicated to Startups and small and medium-sized enterprises (SMEs) with the vision, courage, and determination to take their businesses to the next level.

To the entrepreneurs who work tirelessly to turn their dreams into reality, and the innovators who dare to disrupt and challenge the status quo, this book is for you.

This book would not have been written without the blessings of Shri Salasar Balaji and my adorable parents, Late Shri Bhoj Raj Aggarwal & Smt. Sushila Devi. I am thankful to my loving wife, Kaushal, and my wonderful, lovely children, who have always motivated me to follow my dreams, pursue my passion and do my best.

With lots of love and affection for my grandson Shivansh, I want to thank my entire family, friends, mentors, and associates with great gratitude and humility for their endless love and affection.

With lots & Lots of love & respect,

Thank You,
B M Aggarwal

About This Book

In entrepreneurship, a great idea is only the beginning; you need capital to make your idea a reality. To arrange capital, you must be able to pitch your idea to investors in a way that attracts them to invest. A perfect pitch is the key.

"Pitch Like A Pro: Decoding Investor Pitch" is a guidebook for entrepreneurs, business owners, and professionals looking to improve their pitch. This book provides the information and tools to help you create a pitch that stands out and wins the investor, whether you are looking for venture capital, angel investments, or seed funding.

This book explains how to craft a persuasive and compelling pitch:

1.   The secrets to successful pitching are revealed, starting with understanding your audience and developing a clear value proposition.

2.   You'll learn to craft a compelling opening statement and address risks and challenges.

3.   Learn how to tailor your pitch to your audience and use data and storytelling to engage your audience.

Pitch Like A Pro: Decoding Investor Pitch is written by investors and entrepreneurs who have experienced both the investor side of the pitch. They know what it takes for investors to be interested in your pitch and want more. They are familiar with the positive and negative aspects of pitching and the pitfalls and can help you avoid them.

This book will provide practical advice, real-life examples, and useful tips to help you improve your pitch and take it further. In addition, this book will teach you how to create a pitch that communicates your idea and connects with your audience emotionally.

Pitch Like A Pro: Decoding Investor Pitch is the perfect guide for any entrepreneur, whether experienced or new. This book will help you confidently take your pitch and secure the funding you need to realize your ideas.

Although pitching to investors can seem daunting, with the right approach and a well-crafted pitch, you can secure your business's funding. Entrepreneurs have a vision and passion for their product or service. Therefore, it is important to communicate your passion and vision to potential investors in an easy-to-understand and persuasive manner to win their support.

This book, **Pitch Like A Pro: Decoding Investor Pitch**, will explain how to pitch investors. The principles of effective pitching are the same whether you're a StartUp looking for seed capital or a company in growth seeking venture capital.

We will discuss every aspect of pitching, starting with defining your goals, identifying investors and crafting compelling stories, and delivering flawless pitches. In this book, we will discuss the key components of a winning pitch. This includes developing a clear value proposition, addressing risks and opportunities, providing evidence and supporting data, and concluding with an aggressive call to action.

We will share real-world examples and cautionary tales about pitches that failed. In addition, we will be sharing insights from venture capitalists and experienced entrepreneurs. They will offer practical advice and guidance about creating and delivering winning pitches.

Pitch Like A Pro: Decoding Investor Pitch is more than a book. It's a complete guide that will help you navigate through the complicated world of investor pitching. We hope this book equips you with the knowledge and tools you need to make a compelling pitch to investors that convince them to invest in your business.

If you are ready to take your company to the next level, secure the funding you need, and become professional in pitching, this book will help you.

Brief Introduction to the Author
CA B M Aggarwal

B M Aggarwal, a Chartered Accountant with over 44 years of experience, is a respected figure in finance. He has been active in financial services like project consultancy, loan syndication, loan funding, project financing, project consultancy, and publishing financial periodicals. He is also actively involved in corporate and financial consulting, helping many people and companies reach their financial goals.

His notable accomplishments include his ability to facilitate and advice on IPOs (Initial Public Offerings) for various companies in his role as an IPO advisor. His experience in the finance field and expertise in assisting companies to navigate the complex world of initial public offerings (IPOs) and fundraising speaks volumes.

B M Aggarwal has is on a mission to help 10,000 entrepreneurs scale their businesses and increase their profits through SME IPOs. His dedication to assisting others to succeed in finance and business is evident.

Chapter 1
What Investors Want to See

As an entrepreneur, when preparing for an investor pitch, you must clearly understand what investors are looking for. Investors receive numerous pitch decks every day, and they are looking for specific qualities in a startup before they make an investment. Understanding what investors want to see can help you tailor your pitch to their preferences and increase your chances of success.

This chapter will explore the key aspects investors want to see in a startup pitch. From market analysis to financial projections, we will delve into each element and provide insights on showcasing your startup in the best light possible. Whether preparing for your first pitch or your tenth, this chapter will help you understand what investors are looking for and how you can present your startup as an attractive investment opportunity.

Understanding Investor Priorities:

To successfully secure funding, startups must understand

what investors are looking for. Investors receive numerous pitches from entrepreneurs and need to make decisions quickly and efficiently. Therefore, startups need to tailor their pitches to address investors' priorities.

One of the primary priorities for investors is the growth potential. They want to see that a startup has a scalable business model and the ability to grow rapidly. This requires startups to demonstrate a clear understanding of their target market and a plan for reaching and acquiring new customers. In addition, investors want to see a clear path to revenue growth and profitability.

In addition, investors invest in people as much as they invest in ideas. Thus, the quality of the team is another key priority for investors. They want to see a talented and experienced team with a track record of success. Therefore, startups should highlight the strengths and accomplishments of their team members in their pitch, including educational backgrounds, work experience, and any awards or accolades they have received.

Investors also place a high value on the uniqueness and innovation of a startup's product or service. As a result, startups need to explain how their product or service differs from others on the market and what makes it unique. They should also be able to explain how their product or service solves a real problem and why customers will choose their product over others.

Another important factor for investors is the market size and potential. They want to see a startup targeting a large and growing market. They also want to see that the startup has a plan for how they will capture market share and grow their customer base.

Investors also want to see a clear and realistic financial plan. Startups need to be able to demonstrate how they will generate revenue and how they will use the funding they receive. Investors want to see that a startup has a solid understanding of its costs and margins and that they have a plan for how it will achieve profitability.

Investors want to see that a startup has a clear and well-defined strategy for growth. This means that startups need to have a plan for how they will scale their business and what milestones they will achieve along the way. Investors want to see that a startup has a clear roadmap for growth and that they are committed to achieving its goals.

To address these priorities in your pitch, it is essential to research the investors you will be pitching to. You should understand their investment focus and criteria, as well as their portfolio of investments. This will allow you to customize your pitch to highlight the areas that are most important to them.

Startups should also be prepared to provide detailed information on their business model, market opportunity, team, and financial projections. It is important to be transparent and provide realistic projections, as investors will see through any overinflated claims.

Furthermore, startups should showcase their product or service and explain how it solves a real customer problem. This should be done clearly and concisely to highlight the unique features and benefits of the product or service.

Understanding investors' priorities is critical for any startup looking to secure funding. By tailoring your pitch to address these priorities, you will increase your chances of success and demonstrate your understanding of what it takes to build a successful startup.

The Importance of Market Size:

The market size is a critical factor that investors consider when evaluating a startup. This is because investors seek a significant return on their investment, which can only be achieved if the startup operates in a large and growing market. Therefore, entrepreneurs must conduct extensive market research and provide supporting data to demonstrate the market's potential and the opportunities it presents for growth.

In addition to providing data on the target market's size, growth rate, and trends, entrepreneurs must also provide a clear and compelling value proposition that addresses a significant pain point for their target market. This value proposition must demonstrate that there is a significant demand for the product or service and that it has the potential to capture a significant share of the market.

Investors also prefer startups operating in a market with a high growth potential. Therefore, entrepreneurs should provide data demonstrating the market's potential growth and the opportunities it presents for their startup. This can be achieved by using data on the adoption rate of similar products or services in other markets or industries and emerging trends that are likely to drive growth in the target market.

It is also crucial for entrepreneurs to demonstrate their intense concentration on their work, understanding of the market, and the needs of their target customers. To do this, entrepreneurs can provide data on customer surveys, focus groups, or interviews that they have conducted, as well as feedback from early customers or beta testers.

Understanding the importance of market size and how to demonstrate the potential of the market is crucial for entrepreneurs seeking investment. By conducting extensive market research, providing a clear and compelling value proposition, and demonstrating a deep understanding of the market and the needs of their target customers, entrepreneurs can increase their chances of securing investment from investors.

Addressing the Competition:

When pitching to investors, addressing the competition and explaining what sets your startup apart is crucial. To do this effectively, you need a clear understanding of your competition and your competitive advantage.

Start by identifying your competitors and their offerings to understand the market landscape. Then, demonstrate what makes your startup unique and more likely to succeed than your competitors. This can be based on factors such as unique technology, superior customer service, a strong brand, or a better pricing strategy. Finally, use data and statistics to support your claims and show how your competitive advantage can translate into revenue and growth for your startup.

In addition to demonstrating your competitive advantage, you should identify and be transparent about potential threats and risks. Investors want to see that you have a solid plan to mitigate risks and address threats your competitors pose. It's also important to showcase your market potential and provide evidence of your ability to capture a significant share of the market. Use market research and data to support your claims and build a compelling narrative highlighting your strengths and potential for success.

However, it's important to strike the right balance between confidence and humility. Avoid coming across as arrogant or dismissive of your competitors, and focus on building a narrative that highlights your strengths while being transparent about potential risks and challenges. Addressing the competition is a critical aspect of investor pitching, and by adhering to these principles, you can enhance the likelihood of obtaining investment.

The Value Proposition:

The value proposition is a critical component of any investor pitch. It is a statement that communicates the unique value that a startup's product or service offers to its target customers. The value proposition should explain how the product or service solves a significant problem or meets a crucial need for the customer. It should also highlight the product or service's benefits and what sets it apart from the competition.

Entrepreneurs must first understand their target customers and pain points to communicate the value proposition to investors effectively. Entrepreneurs must know what their customers want and what problems they are trying to solve. Based on this understanding, they can create a value proposition that speaks directly to customers' needs and desires.

The value proposition should be clear, concise, and easy to understand. It should use simple language and avoid technical jargon that may confuse investors. It should also be backed up by data and evidence supporting the statement's claims.

One effective way to communicate the value proposition is through storytelling. Entrepreneurs can use real-life examples and anecdotes to illustrate how their product or service solves a particular problem or meets a specific need. This approach can help investors connect emotionally with the value proposition and understand its real-world impact.

Another effective way to communicate the value proposition is through visuals. For example, entrepreneurs can use diagrams, charts, or infographics to illustrate the key benefits of the product or service and how it solves the customer's problem. This approach can make the value proposition more engaging and memorable for investors.

The value proposition is critical to any investor pitch. It communicates the unique value that a startup's product or service offers to its target customers. To communicate the value proposition effectively, entrepreneurs must understand their target customers, use clear and concise language, back up claims with data and evidence, and use storytelling or visuals to make the value proposition engaging and memorable for investors.

Financial Projections:

Financial projections are crucial to any startup pitch, as investors want to see a clear path to profitability and return on investment. To create realistic financial projections, entrepreneurs need to deeply understand their business model, market potential, and operating costs.

The first step in creating financial projections is to understand your business model comprehensively. This includes understanding your revenue streams, cost structure, and customer acquisition strategy. Next, entrepreneurs should be able to articulate how their startup creates value for its customers and how that value translates into revenue.

Once you clearly understand your business model, you can begin to create financial projections. Investors want to see a clear and concise financial model that shows how your startup will generate revenue, manage costs, and achieve profitability. This model should include revenue projections, operating expenses, capital expenditures, and cash flow projections.

Revenue projections are a critical component of your financial model. They should be based on realistic assumptions about your market potential, customer acquisition strategy, and pricing. Investors want to see that you clearly understand your market and have a realistic plan for capturing a significant share of it.

Operating expenses are another essential component of your financial model. You should clearly understand your fixed and variable costs and how they will impact your profitability. It is also important to factor in costs associated with hiring employees, developing your product or service, and marketing and advertising.

Capital expenditures are another important consideration when creating financial projections. These are the costs associated with acquiring assets, such as equipment or office space, that will be used to generate revenue. Investors want to see that you have a clear plan for managing these costs and that you are not over-investing in assets that will not generate a sufficient return on investment.

Cash flow projections are also critical when creating financial projections. Investors want to see that you have a clear plan for managing your cash flow and that you have a realistic plan for raising capital if necessary. Therefore, cash flow projections should include projections for revenue, expenses, and capital expenditures, as well as an analysis of your burn rate and cash runway.

When creating financial projections, it is important to be conservative and realistic. Investors want to see that you have a clear plan for achieving profitability and factored in potential challenges and risks. It is also important to clearly explain your assumptions and be transparent about any uncertainties or unknowns.

In addition to creating realistic financial projections, entrepreneurs should also be prepared to answer questions about their financials during the pitching process. Investors will want to see that you have a deep understanding of your financials and that you can articulate how your startup will achieve profitability and return on investment.

Overall, financial projections are a critical component of any startup pitch. They should be based on realistic assumptions, conservative estimates, and a deep understanding of your business model and market potential. Entrepreneurs should be prepared to answer questions about their financials and clearly explain their assumptions and projections. By creating realistic financial projections and articulating a clear path to profitability, entrepreneurs can increase their chances of securing investment from investors.

The Team:

When pitching to investors, showcasing the expertise and experience of your team is a critical component of your pitch. Investors invest not just in the product or service but also in the team behind it, as they believe that the success of a startup is highly dependent on the team's ability to execute the plan.

First and foremost, it is essential to introduce your team and highlight their relevant experience and qualifications. Start with the key players, such as the CEO, CTO, and CFO, and then introduce the rest of the team. Include their professional backgrounds, previous positions held, and any notable achievements. This information should be brief and to the point, highlighting the most relevant and impressive aspects of their experience.

It is also important to demonstrate how the team's expertise and experience relate to the startup's product or service. Explain how each team member's skills and experience will contribute to the success of the startup. For example, if your startup is a software company, highlight the relevant experience of your team in software development, user interface design, and customer experience management.

Another way to showcase your team's expertise is to discuss the unique skills and talents each team member brings. Highlight any specializations, certifications, or awards that they have received. This demonstrates to investors that your team has the skills to execute the startup's goals.

In addition to highlighting your team's qualifications, showing that your team is committed to the startup's success is essential. Investors want to see that your team is willing to put in the time and effort required to make the startup successful. Highlight any sacrifices or risks your team has taken to pursue the startup, such as quitting a well-paying job or investing their money in the venture.

Another way to demonstrate your team's commitment is to highlight prior working experience. If some members of your team have worked together before, this shows that they have already built a level of trust and collaboration that can benefit the startup. On the other hand, if your team is new to each other, explaining how you have built a cohesive team and what steps you have taken to ensure effective collaboration can be helpful.

It is essential to communicate your team's vision for the startup. Investors want to see that your team is aligned and has a shared vision for the future of the startup. Discuss your team's goals and objectives for the startup and how you plan to achieve them. Show how your team's expertise and experience are uniquely positioned to execute this vision.

Showcasing your team's expertise and experience is critical to a successful pitch. Introduce your team and highlight their relevant experience and qualifications, demonstrate how their skills and experience relate to the startup's product or service, discuss the unique skills and talents of each team member, show your team's commitment to the startup's success, communicate your team's vision for the startup, and highlight any prior experience working together. By effectively communicating your team's expertise and experience, you can increase your chances of securing investment from investors.

Demonstrating Traction:

Demonstrating traction is a critical aspect of any startup pitch. Investors want to see evidence that a startup is progressing and gaining market traction. This indicates that the startup has a viable product or service that is solving a real problem and that there is a demand for it. There are several ways that startups can demonstrate traction to investors:

1. **User Acquisition and Retention**: One of the most important metrics that investors look at is user acquisition and retention. Startups need to show that they are acquiring new users and retaining existing ones. This can be done by providing data on the number of users, their demographics, and how they use the product or service. Startups can also provide data on user engagement, such as how often users use the product or service and how much time they spend on it.

2. **Revenue Growth:** Investors want to see evidence of revenue growth. Startups can show this by providing data on revenue, including how much revenue has been generated, the revenue model, and any revenue projections. Startups can also provide data on the average revenue per user and how revenue has grown over time.

3. **Partnerships and Collaborations:** Startups can also demonstrate traction by showing partnerships and collaborations with other companies. This can include partnerships with suppliers, distributors, or other companies in the same industry. These partnerships show that the startup is gaining traction and that other companies are interested in working with them.

4. **Press Coverage and Awards:** Press coverage and awards are another way to demonstrate traction. Startups can provide information on any press coverage they have received, such as articles in newspapers or magazines. They can also provide information on any awards they have won, such as industry awards or startup competitions.

5. **Product Development and Innovation:** Investors also want to see product development and innovation evidence. Startups can show this by providing information on new product features, upgrades, or enhancements. They can also provide data on user product feedback, including any surveys or focus groups conducted.

When demonstrating traction to investors, startups need to be transparent and provide evidence to support their claims. Startups should also be able to explain what they have learned from their traction metrics and how they plan to use this information to drive growth in the future.

In addition to providing evidence of traction, startups should also be able to show how they plan to use the traction to scale and grow the business. This can include plans for product development, marketing, and user acquisition.

Finally, it is important for startups to be able to explain any challenges they have faced and how they have overcome them. Investors want to see that startups can overcome obstacles and progress, even in adversity.

Demonstrating traction is a critical aspect of any startup pitch. Startups need to show evidence of user acquisition and retention, revenue growth, partnerships, and collaborations, press coverage and awards, and product development and innovation. Startups should be transparent and provide evidence to support their claims. They should also be able to explain what they have learned from their traction metrics and how they plan to use this information to drive growth in the future. By doing so, startups can show investors that they have a viable product or service that is solving a real problem and that there is a demand for it.

Pitching your startup to investors is an exciting but challenging task requiring a well-crafted pitch deck covering all your business's crucial aspects. By understanding what investors want to see, you can tailor your pitch to their expectations and increase your chances of securing funding.

Remember that investors are not only interested in the potential of your product or service but also in the team behind it, your traction, financial projections, and your competitive advantage. Therefore, showcase your team's expertise and experience, demonstrate your startup's progress and growth, and create realistic financial projections.

Additionally, it's important to strike the right balance between confidence and humility when presenting your pitch. Be honest about the challenges and risks your startup faces and highlight your strengths and potential for success.

Keep in mind that investors want to invest in a business they believe will provide a significant return on their investment. Therefore, focus on showing how your startup can generate revenue and grow, and use market research and data to support your claims.

By following these guidelines and addressing what investors want to see, you can increase your chances of impressing investors and securing funding for your startup.

Chapter 2
Identifying Your Target Investor

Understanding Their Needs and Preferences

In the highly competitive world of startup funding, identifying your target investor is crucial. Different investors have different needs, preferences, and investment criteria, and understanding them can significantly increase your chances of securing funding.

Although angel investors, venture capitalists, and corporate investors have distinct requirements, they all share a common objective: to invest in companies that can generate substantial returns on their investment.

To identify your target investor, you need to understand their investment focus, risk appetite, and preferred investment size. You also need to know their industry expertise, geographic focus, and investment stage preferences. Doing so can tailor your pitch and approach to match their needs and increase your chances of securing investment.

Types of Investors:

When seeking investment for your startup, it's important to understand the different types of investors and their unique investment preferences. Angel investors, venture capitalists, and other types of investors have their own goals and requirements, and tailoring your pitch to their needs can greatly increase your chances of securing funding.

Angel investors are typically high-net-worth individuals who invest their own money into early-stage startups. They usually invest smaller amounts compared to venture capitalists, but they may also be more willing to take on higher risks. Angel investors may also offer valuable advice, mentorship, and industry connections to the startups they invest in.

Professional investors managing funds from institutional investors, such as pension funds, endowments, and family offices, are venture capitalists. They usually invest larger amounts than angel investors and are more focused on high-growth startups with a proven business model and a strong potential for profitability. Venture capitalists may also take a more active role in managing the startups they invest in, providing support with strategy, operations, and fundraising.

Other types of investors may include private equity firms, corporate investors, and crowdfunding platforms. Private equity firms typically invest in more established companies with a success and profitability track record. Corporate investors are businesses that make strategic investments in startups to access new markets, products, or technologies. On the other hand, crowdfunding platforms enable startups to raise funds from a large number of individual investors, typically through an online platform.

It's important for startups to understand the differences between these investors because each type may have different investment criteria, expectations, and preferences. For example, angel investors may be more interested in investing in startups that align with their values or interests. At the same time, venture capitalists may be more focused on startups that have the potential to generate significant returns on investment. Startups may also need to consider the stage of their company, the amount of funding they need, and the type of relationship they want with their investors when deciding which type of investor to approach.

Identifying the right type of investor can be critical for the success of a startup. By understanding the differences between angel investors, venture capitalists, and other investors, startups can tailor their pitch and approach to meet their target investors' specific needs and preferences.

Investor Preferences:

When seeking investment, it's important to identify your target investors and understand their preferences for specific types of investments. This knowledge can help you tailor your pitch to their interests and increase your chances of securing funding.

To begin, it's important to research the types of investments that your target investors typically make. For example, angel investors may be more interested in early-stage startups. At the same time, venture capitalists may be more interested in investing in companies with proven business models and a track record of growth.

One way to identify the specific types of investments that your target investors are interested in is to look at their past investments. You can research the companies they've invested in and the industries they focus on to understand their preferences. This information can be found on their websites, social media profiles, or through publicly available databases such as Crunchbase or PitchBook.

Another way to identify investor preferences is to network and speak with other entrepreneurs who have successfully secured funding from your target investors. They may provide valuable insights into what the investor is looking for and how to tailor your pitch to meet their needs.

After thoroughly understanding your investor's preferences, it becomes crucial to customize your pitch accordingly. This entails emphasizing the aspects of your business that align with their interests and addressing any apprehensions they may have. This tailored approach to pitching your startup will increase your chances of securing investment and demonstrate your attention to detail and professionalism. In addition, investors appreciate founders who can demonstrate adaptability and understanding of their needs and preferences. Remember, an investor's decision to invest is not just based on the viability of your business but also their personal preferences and experiences.

For example, if your target investor is interested in companies with a proven track record of growth, you may want to focus on your company's revenue growth and market traction. Alternatively, if your target investor is interested in early-stage startups, you may want to focus on your innovative technology and unique approach to solving a particular problem.

It's also important to consider the format of your pitch. Some investors prefer a more detailed, data-driven approach, while others may be more interested in hearing your personal story and vision for the future. Understanding the preferences of your target investors can help you craft your pitch to their specific needs and increase your chances of success.

In addition to tailoring your pitch to meet your target investor's preferences, it's also important to be transparent and honest about your business's potential risks and challenges. Investors appreciate honesty and are more likely to invest in companies that have a realistic understanding of the obstacles they face.

Ultimately, identifying your target investor and understanding their preferences for specific types of investments is essential to securing funding for your business. By doing your research, tailoring your pitch, and being transparent about potential risks, you can increase your chances of success and build a strong relationship with your investor.

Leveraging Investor Networks:

One of the best ways to find the right investors for your startup is by leveraging investor networks. Investor networks are groups of investors who share information about potential investments and help each other find opportunities. These networks can be invaluable for startup founders who are looking for funding.

There are several different types of investor networks that you can leverage to find the right investors for your startup. One of the most common types of investor networks is angel investor groups. Angel investor groups are made up of individual investors who pool their money together to invest in startups. These groups can be an excellent source of funding for startups because they typically have a lot of experience investing in early-stage companies and can provide valuable mentorship and connections.

Another type of investor network is venture capital firms. Venture capital firms are professional investment firms that pool money from various sources, including institutional investors, wealthy individuals, and corporations, to invest in startups. These firms typically invest in high-growth companies with the potential for significant returns.

In addition to angel investor groups and venture capital firms, there are a variety of other types of investor networks you can leverage to find the right investors for your startup. These may include industry-specific groups, such as healthcare or technology-focused networks, as well as geographic networks, such as regional investment groups.

To leverage investor networks effectively, it is important to understand how they work and how to access them. One of the best ways to access investor networks is by attending events and conferences where investors gather to network and learn about potential investment opportunities. These events may include pitch competitions, industry-specific conferences, and investor forums.

In addition to attending events, there are also a variety of online platforms that can help you connect with investor networks. These platforms may include crowdfunding websites, such as Kickstarter or Indiegogo, and online investment platforms, such as AngelList or SeedInvest. These platforms can be an excellent way to connect with a large number of potential investors quickly and efficiently.

When leveraging investor networks, it is important to approach potential investors professionally and respectfully. This means taking the time to research the investor's background and interests and tailoring your pitch to their specific needs and preferences. It is also important, to be honest and transparent about your startup's strengths and weaknesses and any potential risks or challenges.

In addition to approaching potential investors directly, you can leverage your existing network to connect with investor networks. This may include reaching out to mentors, advisors, or other entrepreneurs in your industry who may have connections to potential investors. By leveraging your existing network, you can tap into a wider pool of potential investors and increase your chances of finding the right match for your startup.

It is important to remember that leveraging investor networks is just one piece of the puzzle when it comes to raising funding for your startup. It is important to have a strong pitch, a solid business plan, and a clear understanding of your market and competition. Combining these elements with an effective strategy for leveraging investor networks can increase your chances of finding the right investors and securing funding for your startup.

Geographic Considerations:

Regarding finding investors for your startup, geographic considerations can play an important role. Depending on your location, you may have access to various investors, each with its own preferences and investment criteria.

One of the first steps in identifying investors interested in startups from your location is to do some research. Start by looking at local news sources, industry publications, and online forums to get a sense of who the major players are in your area. You can also attend local startup events and networking sessions to meet other entrepreneurs and investors.

Once you have a list of potential investors, it's important to research each in more detail. Look at their investment history, portfolio companies, and investment criteria to determine whether they fit your startup well. You can also find out more about their interests and backgrounds to see if any connections make them more likely to invest in your company.

Another important consideration when it comes to geographic considerations is the regulatory environment in your area. Depending on your location, there may be different rules and regulations governing how startups can raise capital and what types of investors are allowed to invest.

Understanding these regulations and working with a lawyer or other professional who can help you navigate the legal landscape is important.

One way to find investors interested in startups from your location is to leverage local investor networks. These networks are often made up of investors with a shared interest in supporting local startups and may be more willing to take a chance on a new company. You can find these networks by attending local startup events, reaching out to local incubators and accelerators, or joining online forums and groups.

Another strategy for identifying local investors is to look at companies that have recently received funding in your area. By researching these companies and the investors who funded them, you may be able to identify other investors who are interested in startups from your location. You can also reach out to these companies and their founders to see if they can provide advice or introductions to potential investors.

It's important to keep in mind that geographic considerations are just one factor to consider when it comes to finding the right investors for your startup. Ultimately, what matters most is finding investors who are a good fit for your company and who share your vision for the future. By doing your research, networking with other entrepreneurs and investors, and leveraging local resources, you will have better chances of finding the right investors for your startup, regardless of where you are located.

Industry Focus:

As a startup founder, one of the critical tasks is to identify and target the right investors for your industry. Investors who have experience or interest in your industry are more likely to understand the unique challenges and opportunities of your business and, therefore, more likely to invest in your startup.

Here are some strategies to identify investors who have

experience or interest in your startup's industry:

1. **Research Industry-Specific Investment Firms:** Many investment firms specialize in specific industries, such as healthcare, technology, or consumer goods. These firms deeply understand the industry, its trends, and its challenges. Researching and identifying these firms can be an effective way to find investors with experience in your industry.

2. **Attend Industry-Specific Conferences and Events:** Attending industry-specific conferences and events can be an excellent way to meet investors who have a vested interest in your industry. These events offer opportunities to network and build relationships with investors, learn about industry trends and challenges, and gain insights into what investors are looking for in startups.

3. **Utilize Industry-Specific Online Communities:** Many industries have online communities and forums to discuss industry-specific topics, trends, and challenges. These communities are a great place to connect with investors interested in your industry, ask questions, and learn about investment opportunities.

4. **Leverage Your Industry Network:** Your network can be a valuable resource for finding investors with experience or interest in your startup's industry. Reach out to colleagues, mentors, and industry experts and ask for introductions to investors who may be a good fit for your startup.

5. **Research Investor Portfolios:** Many investors publicly disclose their investment portfolios on their websites or other public channels. Researching these portfolios can be a good way to identify investors who have already invested in startups in your industry. Once

you have identified these investors, you can introduce your startup.

6. **Identify Industry-Specific Publications:** Industry-specific publications, such as trade journals or industry magazines, often feature articles about active investors in a particular industry. These publications can be a great source of information for identifying investors who have experience or interest in your industry.

7. **Look for Industry-Specific Incubators and Accelerators:** Many incubators and accelerators are industry-specific and focus on startups in a particular industry. These programs offer a range of resources, including mentorship, funding, and networking opportunities, that can be valuable for startups looking to connect with investors interested in their industry.

Identifying investors with experience or interest in your startup's industry is critical for securing funding and building a successful startup. By utilizing the strategies outlined above, you can increase your chances of finding the right investors for your industry and, ultimately, securing your startup's funding to succeed.

Investment Stage:

Understanding the investment stages investors' focus on and tailoring your pitch accordingly is crucial to securing funding for your startup. Additionally, it is crucial to comprehend the varying preferences of investors regarding the investment stage before seeking funding from them.

The most common investment stages are the seed, early, growth, and later stages. Each stage represents a different level of development for a startup and requires different funding. For example, the seed stage is the earliest stage of a startup's growth, while the later stage represents the most mature stage.

Seed-stage startups typically have an idea, a prototype, or a minimum viable product (MVP). They require funding to validate their idea, build their product, and launch it in the market. Seed-stage investors are typically angel investors, friends and family, and early-stage venture capitalists. These investors are willing to take a risk on a startup with a promising idea or a strong founding team.

Early-stage startups have launched their product in the market and are looking to scale, and require funding to hire a team, acquire customers, and grow their business. Early-stage investors are typically venture capitalists and angel investors who specialize in early-stage investments. These investors are looking for startups with a validated product, a growing customer base, and a clear path to revenue.

Growth-stage startups have achieved product-market fit and are looking to expand their business. They require funding to scale their operations, enter new markets, and develop new products. Growth-stage investors are typically late-stage venture capitalists and private equity firms. These investors are looking for startups with a proven business model, a growing customer base, and a clear path to profitability.

Later-stage startups are mature companies looking to raise funding for strategic acquisitions, buyouts, or IPOs. They require funding to fuel their growth and expansion. Later-stage investors are typically private equity firms, hedge funds, and institutional investors. These investors are looking for companies with a proven track record, a stable cash flow, and a strong market position.

To tailor your pitch to the right investor, it is essential to understand the investment stage they focus on. Seed-stage investors are looking for promising ideas and strong founding teams, while early-stage investors are looking for startups with validated products and a growing customer base. Growth-stage investors are looking for companies with a proven business model and a clear path to profitability. Finally, later-stage investors are looking for companies with a stable cash flow and a strong market position.

When pitching to investors, it is essential to communicate your startup's development stage and funding requirements. Investors want to know your startup's stage and how much funding you need to achieve your goals. Therefore, be transparent about your funding requirements and explain how the funding will be used to grow your business.

In addition to understanding the investment stages that investors focus on, it is also essential to understand the terms that investors use to describe their investment preferences. For example, seed-stage investors may describe themselves as pre-seed, seed, or early-stage investors. Early-stage investors may describe themselves as series A, series B, or growth investors.

Understanding these terms can help you identify the right investors for your startup and tailor your pitch accordingly. If you are a seed-stage startup, you should focus on pitching to pre-seed, seed, and early-stage investors. If you are an early-stage startup, you should focus on pitching to series A, series B, or growth investors.

Identifying your target investor is crucial in securing funding for your startup. By understanding potential investors' needs, preferences, and investment criteria, you can tailor your pitch and increase your chances of success. Consider the factors discussed in this chapter, including the types of investors, investor preferences, leveraging investor networks, geographic considerations, and industry focus. By doing so, you can identify the right investors for your startup, build the relationships necessary to secure funding and take your company to the next level.

Investor Profiles:

Creating profiles of your target investors is essential in understanding their needs and preferences. It involves conducting research on the investor to gather information such as their investment history, industry experience, investment focus, and funding preferences. The information gathered can help you create a detailed profile that can be used to craft your pitch and increase your chances of securing investment.

One way to start creating investor profiles is by identifying potential investors through online research or attending networking events. Once you have identified potential investors, you can start gathering information about them by looking at their portfolio companies, investment history, and any news articles or interviews they have given. You can also use online tools such as LinkedIn to gain insights into their background, experience, and interests.

It is essential to keep in mind that investors are unique, and their needs and preferences may differ. Thus, creating individualized profiles for each investor is crucial to understanding their unique investment requirements. You can use a template to structure your profiles, ensuring that you gather all the essential information.

One of the critical pieces of information to include in your investor profile is their investment history. This information can help you understand the types of companies the investor has invested in previously and the amount of funding they typically provide. It can also help you determine the investor's risk appetite and the types of businesses that align with their investment strategies.

Another crucial information to include in your investor profile is their industry experience. Investors with industry experience in your startup's sector can bring valuable knowledge, connections, and insight. In addition, they can help you navigate industry-specific challenges and provide guidance to help your business grow.

Additionally, it is essential to consider the investment focus of the investor. Some investors focus on early-stage startups, while others focus on later-stage companies. Understanding the investment focus of the investor can help you tailor your pitch accordingly, highlighting the aspects of your business that align with their investment criteria.

Lastly, it is essential to consider the funding preferences of the investor. Some investors prefer to invest in companies at specific funding rounds, while others are open to investing at any stage. Knowing the funding preferences of the investor can help you plan your funding strategy and pitch to ensure that you meet their investment criteria.

Creating profiles of your target investors can help you tailor your pitch, understand their investment criteria, and increase your chances of securing investment. By identifying potential investors, researching their investment history, industry experience, investment focus, and funding preferences, you can create a detailed profile that can be used to guide your fundraising efforts. It is essential to keep in mind that investors are unique, and their investment criteria may differ. Thus, creating individualized profiles for each investor is crucial to understanding their unique investment requirements.

Identifying your target investors and understanding their needs and preferences is critical to successfully raising funding for your startup. By taking the time to research and create profiles of potential investors, you can tailor your pitch to better resonate with their interests and increase your chances of securing investment.

Remember, different investors, have different investment preferences, so it's important to understand the differences between angel investors, venture capitalists, and other types of investors. Additionally, leveraging investor networks and geographic considerations can also play a role in identifying the right investors for your startup.

Keep in mind that investors focus on specific investment stages and industries, so understanding your startup's investment stage and tailoring your pitch to align with their interests is crucial. Following these guidelines and continually refining your approach can increase your chances of finding the right investors for your startup and securing the funding you need to grow and succeed.

Chapter 3
Crafting Your Pitch

Key Components and Elements to Include

Crafting a compelling pitch is critical to raising funds for your startup. Whether you seek investment from venture capitalists, angel investors, or crowdfunding platforms, your pitch is your opportunity to showcase your business idea and convince investors that your startup has what it takes to succeed.

A pitch concisely presents your business idea that highlights its key features, benefits, and potential market opportunities. The goal is to communicate your startup's value proposition clearly and compellingly that captures the attention of potential investors.

Creating a successful pitch requires careful planning, preparation, and practice. You need to understand your audience, identify their needs and preferences, and tailor your pitch accordingly. You also need to effectively communicate your vision, strategy, and goals in a persuasive and memorable way.

This chapter will explore the essential elements of a successful pitch and provide tips and best practices for crafting a pitch that resonates with your target investors. Whether you are pitching to a group of seasoned venture capitalists or a crowdfunding audience, this chapter will equip you with the necessary resources to present a persuasive argument for your startup.

The Elevator Pitch:

The elevator pitch is a brief, concise, and impactful pitch that summarizes the key components of your startup in a short time. It's called an elevator pitch because it means you should be able to deliver it during an elevator ride. An elevator pitch aims to attract potential investors and persuade them to delve deeper into your business. The pitch must be succinct, clear, and captivating. Its structure should be designed to seize the listener's attention and stimulate curiosity, compelling them to learn more about your startup. An effective elevator pitch should not exceed 30-60 seconds in duration, and it should answer the following questions:

1. What problem does your startup solve?
2. How does your startup solve that problem?
3. What is your target market?
4. What is the size of the market opportunity?
5. What is your unique value proposition?
6. What is your business model?
7. What is your traction to date?
8. What are you looking for from investors?

When crafting your elevator pitch, it is crucial to prioritize the essential aspects of your business. In addition, you must emphasize the critical elements distinguishing your business from others in the market. This will make you stand out from the competition and make your business more appealing to potential investors.

Using the problem-solution framework is one effective way to structure your elevator pitch. Start by identifying the problem that your startup solves and then explain how your solution solves that problem. For example, let's say your startup has developed a mobile app that assists people in locating parking spots in congested cities. Your elevator pitch could begin with something like this: "Urban parking can be a nightmare, and drivers waste precious time searching for available spots. Our mobile app locates open parking spaces in real-time, making it a convenient solution for city drivers seeking to save time and reduce frustration."

Another effective approach is to use storytelling to engage the listener. Incorporate a personal touch into your pitch by sharing a personal experience or anecdote that inspired you to start the business. This not only helps to establish a human connection between you and the listener but also helps to highlight the problem that your business aims to solve. By explaining how your solution solves the problem that you experienced, you can make your pitch more relatable and memorable to potential investors. This emotional connection can create a lasting impression, making the listener more likely to invest in your business.

When delivering your elevator pitch, being confident and enthusiastic is important. Practice your pitch in front of a mirror or with friends and family to get comfortable with the delivery. You must be capable of adjusting your pitch based on the context and audience. Different investors may be interested in different aspects of your business, so your approach must be flexible and adaptable.

The elevator pitch holds significant importance in your pitch deck and fundraising plan. It must be engaging, clear, and succinct while effectively highlighting the key aspects of your business. You can structure your pitch using storytelling and the problem-solution framework to communicate your message effectively. Being adaptable and practicing your pitch can help you make a strong impression on investors. Ultimately, a well-crafted elevator pitch can be the key to capturing the attention and interest of investors and taking your startup to the next level.

The Problem:

The problem is the first and one of the most critical components of any startup pitch. It is why your startup exists and the pain point you aim to address. By clearly identifying and articulating the problem that your startup solves, investors will be able to understand the value of your solution and the market opportunity it represents.

Find a way to communicate that connects with your audience. This means understanding your target market, their challenges, and how your solution is tailored to their needs.

When describing the problem, it's important to be specific and to provide data to support your claims. For example, suppose you are creating a new software product to streamline the hiring process for small businesses. In that case, small businesses spend an average of 23 hours per hire, and 48% of small business owners say hiring is their biggest challenge. By highlighting these specific pain points, you can help investors understand the magnitude of the problem and the potential market opportunity.

It's also important to demonstrate the urgency of the problem and why it needs to be solved now. This could include discussing recent market trends or changes exacerbating the problem or highlighting the potential consequences of not addressing it. By showing that the problem is significant and urgent, you can help investors understand why your solution is needed and why now is the time to invest in your startup.

In addition to describing the problem, it's also important to provide context around why existing solutions have failed to address it adequately. This could include discussing the limitations of current solutions or highlighting the gaps in the market that your solution fills. By doing so, you can help investors understand why your solution is uniquely positioned to address the problem and why it has the potential to disrupt the market.

When crafting your pitch, it's important to remember that investors are looking for startups that can provide a significant return on their investment. By effectively communicating the problem that your startup solves, you can demonstrate that there is a significant market opportunity and that your solution has the potential to generate substantial returns. In addition, by highlighting the problem's urgency, you can create momentum and urgency around your solution, which can help attract investors looking for high-growth opportunities.

The problem is a critical component of any startup pitch. To effectively communicate the problem, you need to clearly articulate it in a way that resonates with your audience, demonstrate the urgency of the problem, and provide context around why existing solutions have failed to address it adequately. By doing so, you can help investors understand the market opportunity and the potential for your solution to generate significant returns.

The Solution:

The solution is the heart of any startup pitch. It is the part where you explain how your company solves your identified problem. This is the section where you demonstrate your company's unique value proposition and differentiate yourself from your competitors. Therefore, it's essential to clearly explain how your solution addresses the problem and why it's better than what is currently available.

One effective way to explain your solution is by using a story. Start with a relatable problem that your target customers face, and then introduce your solution as the hero that comes to their rescue. This approach helps investors to understand your solution easily.

Another effective way to communicate your solution is through a product demonstration. A physical product can be shown to the investors and let them experience it for themselves. If you have a digital product, you can provide a demo or video showcasing its work. This approach can help investors understand your solution's value and see how it works in practice.

Make sure that your solution is easy to understand and not too complex. If your solution is too complicated or technical, it may be difficult for investors to understand, and they may lose interest. Use simple language and avoid industry jargon as much as possible. Showcase the benefits of your solution rather than the technical details.

It's also important to explain how your solution differs from other options. For example, what makes your solution unique? What is your unique selling proposition (USP)? Make sure that you clearly articulate how your solution is better than what is currently available and why customers would choose your product over your competitors.

If you have any intellectual property (IP), such as patents or trademarks, highlight them. Investors are always looking for companies with strong IP protection, as it can give them a competitive advantage in the market.

Finally, it's important to show that you have a clear roadmap for developing and improving your solution. Explain how you plan to develop your solution over time and what new features or improvements you plan to make. This will show that you have a long-term vision for your company and are committed to continuous improvement.

The solution section of your pitch is where you explain how

your company solves the problem you have identified. Use a story or a product demonstration to explain your solution in a way that is easy to understand. Clearly articulate your unique selling proposition and how your solution is better than currently available. Highlight any intellectual property and show you have a clear roadmap for developing and improving your solution.

The Market:

In crafting a pitch for your startup, one of the most critical elements is demonstrating a clear understanding of your target market and the opportunity within that market. In addition, investors want to see that you have a solid plan for reaching your target customers and that there exists enough demand for your product or service.

The initial step in showcasing the market potential for your startup is to understand your target market, which is a specific group of potential customers who can be most likely to be interested in your product or service. Identifying your target market early in your startup's development is crucial, as it will inform a range of decisions, such as product development, marketing tactics, and sales strategies. Consider the following factors to identify market demand:

1. **Demographics:** Start by defining the characteristics of your ideal customer. What is their age group, gender, income level, and geographic location? Demographic information will help you understand the size and scope of your target market.

2. **Needs and Behaviors:** What are the needs and behaviors of your ideal customer and their problems that your product or service can solve? Understanding these factors will help you develop a product suitable for your target market.

3. **Competitors:** Who are your competitors, and how are they serving the needs of your target market? What gaps exist in the market that your product or service can fill? Identifying these gaps will help you position your product in the market.

Having identified your target market, the next step is to demonstrate the market opportunity for your startup. Investors want to see that there is a significant demand for your product or service and that you have a solid plan for reaching your target customers. Tips for effectively communicating the market opportunity for your startup:

1. **Market Size:** Start by quantifying the size of your target market. How big is your target market? What is the total market size in terms of revenue?

2. **Market Growth:** What is the expected growth rate of your target market? Is the market expanding or contracting? Understanding the growth potential of your target market is essential in demonstrating the market opportunity for your startup.

3. **Market Segmentation:** Break down your target market into specific segments based on demographics, needs, behaviors, or other relevant factors. This will help you understand your target market's different sub-markets and how to target each segment effectively.

4. **Competitive Landscape**: Analyze your competitors and their market share. What is your competitive advantage, and how will you differentiate your product or service? Understanding the competitive landscape is critical in demonstrating the market opportunity for your startup.

5. **Customer Acquisition:** Finally, demonstrate your plan for acquiring customers. How will you reach your target customers, and what marketing and sales strategies will you use? Investors want to see that you

have a solid plan for acquiring customers and growing your market share.

Understanding your target market and the market opportunity for your startup is critical in crafting an effective pitch for investors. Take time to identify your target market and analyze the market opportunity, including the size, growth potential, segmentation, competitive landscape, and customer acquisition strategies. By demonstrating a clear understanding of your market, you can help investors see the potential for your startup and increase your chances of securing funding.

The Business Model:

The business model is a crucial aspect of any startup pitch. It outlines how a company generates revenue and creates value for its customers. A well-defined business model helps investors understand how a startup intends to make money and provides a clear roadmap for the company's growth and success.

When crafting your pitch, it's essential to clearly articulate your business model and how it fits into your overall strategy. Various business models exist, such as subscription-based, advertising-based, transaction-based, and commission-based models. The selection should be based on the startup's objectives, product, and target market.

One common type of business model is the subscription-based model, where customers pay a recurring fee to access a product or service. This model is popular among software-as-a-service (SaaS) companies, such as Dropbox and Adobe, where users pay a monthly or yearly subscription fee to access their products. The subscription model provides predictable revenue and creates a loyal customer base.

Another business model is the advertising-based model, where companies generate revenue by displaying ads to their users. Social media platforms like Facebook and Twitter commonly use this model. The key to this model is to have a large user base and the ability to target ads effectively to increase the chances of users clicking on them.

A transaction-based model is another popular model, where companies earn revenue by taking a commission on every transaction that takes place on their platform. E-commerce platforms like Amazon and eBay commonly use this model. These companies generate revenue by taking a small percentage of each sale while providing a valuable service to their customers.

Please note that there is no one-size-fits-all business model, and the right model for your startup depends on various factors such as your product, market, and customer needs. The key is to understand your customers' needs and pain points and choose a model that provides value to them while generating revenue for your business.

When presenting your business model in your pitch, it's crucial to be clear and concise. Start by describing your target market and the problem your product or service solves. Then, explain how your business model generates revenue and creates customer value. Finally, use examples to illustrate how your business model has worked in the past or how it compares to similar companies in your market.

Address any potential concerns or risks associated with your business model. For example, investors will want to know if there are any barriers to entry, potential regulatory issues, or if the model is sustainable over the long term. By anticipating and addressing these concerns, you can instill confidence in your investors and demonstrate your understanding of your market and industry.

The business model is critical to any startup pitch. It outlines how a company generates revenue and creates value for its customers. When presenting your business model, choosing the right model that aligns with your startup's goals, product, and market is essential. Be clear and concise, use examples, and address any potential concerns or risks associated with your model. Doing this can demonstrate your market understanding, build investor confidence, and set your startup up for success.

The Traction:

When pitching to investors, demonstrating traction is essential. Traction is a measure of your startup's progress in gaining customers, generating revenue, and building a user base. It is an important indicator of your startup's potential for success and a key factor in convincing investors to invest in your business.

There are several ways to demonstrate traction to investors. The first is to provide data that shows your startup's growth over time. This might include metrics such as monthly active users, customer acquisition cost, or revenue growth. Investors want to see that your startup is gaining momentum and that there is a clear path to growth in the future.

Another way to demonstrate traction is to provide case studies or testimonials from satisfied customers. This can help investors understand your startup's value and its impact on its customers. It can also show that your startup clearly understands its target market and is meeting the needs of its customers.

If your startup has received any industry awards or recognition, this can also be a great way to demonstrate traction. It shows that your startup is gaining recognition in the industry. This can be particularly effective if the awards or recognition are from reputable sources.

Another way to demonstrate traction is to show that your startup has attracted top talent or strategic partners. This can indicate that your startup is viewed as a leader in the industry and has the potential for long-term success.

Demonstrating traction is about showing investors that your startup is making progress and has the potential for long-term success. By providing data, case studies, testimonials, industry recognition, and strategic partnerships, you can build a compelling case for why investors should invest in your business.

It is important to note that while demonstrating traction is important, it is not the only factor that investors consider when evaluating startups. Investors also look at the quality of the team, the strength of the business model, and the competitive landscape, among other factors. However, demonstrating traction can be a powerful way to build credibility and confidence with investors and can help your startup stand out in a crowded field.

To effectively demonstrate traction, you must clearly understand your startup's key performance indicators (KPIs). KPIs are the metrics that you use to measure the progress and success of your startup. Of course, they can vary depending on the nature of your business. Still, they might include metrics such as monthly recurring revenue (MRR), customer acquisition cost (CAC), customer lifetime value (CLTV), or user engagement metrics.

Once you have identified your KPIs, it is important to track them consistently over time and present them clearly and compellingly to investors. This might involve creating a dashboard or visual representation of your KPIs that you can share with investors during your pitch.

It is important to be transparent about any challenges or setbacks your startup has experienced. Investors understand that building a startup is challenging, and they want to see that you can navigate these challenges effectively. By being honest and transparent about your startup's journey, you can build trust with investors and show them that you are resilient and committed to the success of your business.

Demonstrating traction is critical to a successful pitch to investors. By providing data, case studies, testimonials, industry recognition, and strategic partnerships, you can show investors that your startup is progressing and has the potential for long-term success. In addition, it is important to clearly understand your startup's KPIs, track them consistently over time, and be transparent about any challenges or setbacks that your startup has experienced.

The Team:

When pitching to investors, one key element that can make or break a startup's chances of success is the team. Investors want to know that the startup they are investing in has a strong and capable team that can execute the business plan and take the company to the next level. As a result, it is important for founders to spend time highlighting the expertise and experience of their team during the pitch.

First and foremost, it is important to introduce the key members of the team and their roles within the company. This should include the founders and key executives, such as the Chief Technology Officer or Chief Marketing Officer. Founders should also highlight any advisors or mentors who are involved with the company and can provide guidance and support.

Next, it is important to emphasize the relevant experience of each team member. This includes their past work experience and education and other relevant skills or expertise they bring to the table. Founders should also highlight any relevant accomplishments or successes that the team members have achieved in the past, such as launching successful products or winning industry awards.

In addition to experience and expertise, investors also want to see that the team is capable of working together effectively. This means highlighting any collaborative efforts or successful team projects that have been completed in the past. Founders should also discuss how the team communicates and works together on a day-to-day basis, highlighting any specific strategies or tools that are used to ensure effective collaboration.

Another key aspect of the team that investors will be looking at is the team's commitment to the startup. This means demonstrating that the team is passionate about the company's mission and willing to go above and beyond to ensure its success. Founders should discuss team members' sacrifices to be part of the startup, such as taking a pay cut or working long hours. This can help investors feel more confident in the team's commitment to the company's success.

It is important to discuss any plans for expanding the team. This could include plans to hire additional team members in key areas, such as sales or engineering. Founders should discuss how they plan to recruit new team members and what criteria they will use to evaluate potential candidates. This can help investors feel more confident in the startup's ability to scale and grow.

The team is a critical element of any startup pitch. By highlighting the expertise and experience of the team, as well as their ability to work together effectively and their commitment to the company's success, founders can help investors feel more confident in the startup's ability to execute its business plan and achieve success in the market.

The Financials:

Your startup's financials are an essential part of your pitch when seeking investment from potential investors. Investors want to know that their investment will be used effectively and generate a return. Therefore, it's crucial to create realistic financial projections that demonstrate the financial viability of your startup.

When creating financial projections, it's essential to be realistic and conservative. Investors are wary of overly optimistic projections that do not take into account potential challenges or market fluctuations. Therefore, it's important to base your projections on sound assumptions and research. You should also be transparent about any potential risks or uncertainties that may impact your financials.

Your financial projections should include several key elements, including revenue, cost, and cash flow projections. Revenue projections should outline your expected revenue streams, including the sources of revenue and the projected revenue growth rate. Cost projections should detail your expected expenses, including fixed and variable costs, and the projected cost growth rate. Cash flow projections should show how your startup will generate positive cash flow and when you expect to achieve profitability.

In addition to financial projections, you should also be able to demonstrate the financial viability of your startup. This means showcasing how your startup plans to generate revenue and achieve profitability. You should also be able to articulate how you plan to use the investment funds and how they will contribute to the financial success of your startup.

It's important to note that investors will also be interested in your financial track record. This means providing information about your past financial performance, including revenue growth, profitability, and notable financial achievements. Investors will also be interested in your financial management capabilities, including your ability to manage cash flow and control expenses.

When presenting your financials, it's important to be clear and concise. Use visuals, such as charts and graphs, to help illustrate your projections and make them easier to understand. You should also be prepared to answer questions and provide additional information if requested.

The financials are a crucial component of your pitch to potential investors. It's essential to create realistic financial projections that demonstrate the financial viability of your startup. Additionally, you should be able to articulate how you plan to use the investment funds and how they will contribute to the financial success of your startup. By presenting clear and concise financials, you can increase your chances of securing investment and achieving success in your startup venture.

The Ask:

Asking for funding from investors is a critical component of any startup pitch. While the other elements of the pitch are essential for demonstrating the value of your startup, the ask is where you make your request for funding and show investors what they will get in return for their investment. Therefore, creating a clear and concise ask that accurately reflects your startup's funding needs and aligns with your target investors' interests is essential.

The first step in creating a compelling ask is determining the specific funding amount you need. This can be based on your financial projections and the milestones you need to achieve in the short and long term. Be clear about the funding you require and avoid vague requests that may give investors the impression that you need clarification on your financial needs. Remember to ask for enough funding to achieve your goals, but not so much that it raises questions about the financial viability of your startup.

Once you have determined the amount of funding you need, explaining how you plan to use the funds is essential. This should align with the milestones you need to achieve and demonstrate to investors that you have a clear plan for achieving your goals. For example, if you plan to use the funds to hire additional staff, be specific about the roles you need to fill and the skills required for those roles. If you plan to use the funds to develop new products, explain how this will be accomplished and the potential market for those products.

It is also important to be transparent about the risks associated with your ask. Investors are aware that startups are risky investments, and they want to see that you have thought about the potential risks and have a plan to mitigate them. Therefore, be honest about the challenges you may face and the steps you plan to take to overcome those challenges. This shows investors that you are aware of the potential risks and are prepared to address them.

In addition to the amount of funding and the use of funds, it is important to explain the terms of your ask. This includes the equity stake you are offering in return for the investment, the valuation of your startup, and any other terms that may be relevant. Investors want to see that you have thought about the terms of your ask and that they are fair and reasonable.

When making your ask, it is important to be confident and clear in your delivery. It's crucial to rehearse your pitch beforehand and anticipate potential inquiries that investors may have. Moreover, it's essential to maintain flexibility and be receptive to potential alterations to your pitch based on the feedback you receive from investors. Additionally, it's important to remain open to negotiating terms with investors to create a mutually beneficial partnership. Investors may have suggestions or ideas that can help you improve your pitch or refine your funding strategy, so be open to feedback and willing to adapt your approach.

Remember that the ask is not just about the money. It is also about the relationship you are building with investors. Take the time to understand their needs and interests, and tailor your ask accordingly. By demonstrating that you understand their perspective and are committed to building a long-term relationship, you can create a sense of trust and confidence that can help you secure the funding you need to grow your startup.

The ask is a critical component of any startup pitch. It is important to be clear and concise about the funding you need, the use of funds, the terms of your request, and the risks associated with it. Be confident in your delivery, flexible in your approach, and open to feedback from investors. By building a strong relationship with investors and demonstrating your commitment to achieving your goals, you can create a compelling ask that can help you secure the funding you need to grow your startup.

The Exit Strategy:

When investors put their money into a startup, they expect a return on their investment at some point in the future. As such, startups need a clear plan for investors to exit their investments and realize their returns.

There are several ways in which investors can exit their investment, including a sale of the company, an initial public offering (IPO), or a buyback by the company. All these options have advantages and disadvantages, and the choice will depend on the company's goals and the preferences of the investors.

A sale of the company is a common exit strategy for investors. This can be achieved by selling the company to another business in the same industry or a private equity firm. In such cases, the investors receive a return on their investment based on the company's sale price. This exit strategy is often preferred by investors looking for a quick return on their investment and not interested in holding onto their shares for the long term.

An IPO is another option for investors to exit their

investments. This involves taking the company public and listing its shares on a stock exchange. This allows investors to sell their shares on the open market, providing them with liquidity and the ability to realize their returns. An IPO is typically a longer-term exit strategy, and it requires a significant amount of capital and time to achieve.

A buyback by the company is another option for investors to exit their investments. This involves the company repurchasing shares from the investors at a predetermined price. This option can be attractive to investors looking for a guaranteed return on their investment and are not interested in the risks associated with an IPO or a sale of the company.

Startups need to have a clear plan for their exit strategy from the outset. This helps to provide investors with a clear understanding of how they can realize their returns and the potential timeframe for doing so. A clear exit strategy can also attract investors looking for a specific type of investment opportunity and help align the startup's and its investors' interests.

The exit strategy is critical to a startup's pitch to investors. Demonstrating a clear plan for how investors can exit their investments and realize their returns can help to attract investors and align the interests of the startup and its investors. Startups should consider the advantages and disadvantages of each exit strategy and choose the one that best aligns with their goals and the preferences of their investors.

Crafting a pitch that effectively communicates the key components of your startup is essential to securing funding from investors. In this chapter, we discussed the key elements that should be included in your pitch: the problem your startup solves, your unique solution, your target market, your business model, traction, team, financials, ask, and exit strategy.

We also highlighted the importance of tailoring your pitch to your audience and creating a clear and compelling narrative that captures the attention of potential investors. Finally, remember to practice your pitch and incorporate feedback from others to continually improve and refine your message.

Crafting a successful pitch takes time, effort, and careful consideration of your audience and your startup's unique value proposition. By following the guidelines outlined in this chapter, you can create a pitch that effectively communicates your startup's potential and attracts the attention and investment of key stakeholders.

Ultimately, a successful pitch is about more than just securing funding. It's about creating a compelling vision for your startup and inspiring others to join you on the journey to success. You can build a strong foundation for long-term growth and success with a well-crafted pitch and a clear understanding of your startup's value proposition.

Chapter 4
Perfecting Your Pitch Delivery
Techniques to Enhance Presentation Skills

The preceding chapter explored the fundamental components and critical elements required to craft a compelling pitch deck that effectively communicates your Startup's value proposition. However, creating an exceptional pitch deck alone does not guarantee success in securing funding from investors. The delivery of your pitch is as significant as its content. Regardless of how innovative and promising your StartUp idea is, if your delivery falls short, you risk losing the attention and interest of potential investors.

This chapter is focused on enhancing your presentation skills and refining your pitch delivery. We will examine techniques encompassing body language, tone of voice, pacing, and slide design. In this chapter, you will have access to a comprehensive toolkit that will enable you to deliver a refined and engaging pitch that captivates the attention and interest of investors. So let's dive in and explore the strategies to perfect your pitch delivery.

Importance of Delivery:

Effective delivery is crucial to any pitch, whether to potential investors, customers, or partners. While a well-crafted pitch is essential to the equation, how you deliver it can be equally important. A poor delivery can undermine the strongest pitch, while a confident and engaging delivery can elevate an average pitch.

When pitching the investors to secure funding for your StartUp, the importance of delivery cannot be overstated. Investors are not only looking for a good idea; they want to see that the entrepreneur is passionate, confident, and capable of executing the plan. Your delivery can convey your expertise, professionalism, and belief in your idea, which can play a crucial role in whether or not investors decide to invest in your StartUp.

Investors are also looking to establish a connection with the entrepreneurs they are considering investing in. Presenting your pitch clearly and engagingly establishes rapport with potential investors and builds trust and mutual understanding. This can be even more important, especially in the early fundraising stages when you seek to establish relationships and build a network of supporters.

Additionally, your delivery can help your StartUp stand out from the crowd. Investors hear dozens or even hundreds of pitches, many of which may be similar. By delivering your pitch uniquely and memorably, you can help your StartUp stand out and increase your chances of securing funding.

Delivering your pitch is critical because it shows your enthusiasm and dedication toward the project and can impact your fundraising efforts' success. By perfecting your delivery skills, you can increase your chances of success and maximize the potential of your StartUp. In addition, effective delivery can convey your expertise, professionalism, and confidence in your idea, establish a connection with your investors, and help you stand out.

Body Language and Vocal Delivery:

When it comes to delivering an effective pitch, body language, and vocal delivery are two key components that can make or break your presentation. Even if you have a compelling pitch deck and a great idea, if your body language and vocal delivery are lacking, it can be challenging to capture the attention and interest of your audience, particularly investors.

Body language refers to non-verbal cues to convey meaning, emotions, and thoughts. In a pitch setting, it includes everything from our posture and facial expressions to our gestures and eye contact. Research has shown that body language can account for up to 55% of the message we convey, while vocal delivery accounts for 38%, leaving only 7% for the actual content of our words.

Therefore, paying attention to your body language and best using it to your advantage when delivering a pitch is essential. Regarding body language, your posture is one of the most important aspects. For example, standing straight with your shoulders back, chest out, and head held high can convey confidence and authority, while slouching or hunching over can make you appear timid or unsure. Additionally, maintaining eye contact with your audience can help establish trust and rapport, while looking down or avoiding eye contact can be interpreted as a lack of confidence or dishonesty.

Another crucial aspect of body language is facial expressions. Smiling and making positive facial expressions can help you establish a connection with your investors and convey enthusiasm for your idea. However, remember not to overdo it or come across as insincere. It's also essential to be aware of any nervous habits or tics, such as fidgeting or touching your hair or face. These can be distracting and spoil the overall impact of your pitch.

In addition to body language, vocal delivery is another critical component of an effective pitch. Vocal delivery refers to how we use our voice to convey meaning, tone, and emotion. It includes everything from the pace and volume of our speech to our tone and inflection.

One technique to enhance your vocal delivery is to use variation in the pace and tone of your speech. Speaking at a monotone or consistent pace can be boring and make it difficult for your audience to stay engaged. Instead, try varying the pace of your speech to emphasize certain points and keep your audience interested. Similarly, using different tones and inflections can help convey emotion and enthusiasm for your idea.

You must be aware of your volume and projection. Speaking too softly or too loudly distracts and makes it difficult for the audience to follow along. A good rule of thumb is to speak slightly louder than your normal voice and to project your voice to the back of the room so that everyone can hear you.

Another vocal delivery technique is pauses and emphasis to emphasize key points. Pausing before or after an important point can help your audience absorb the information and give it time to sink in. Emphasizing certain words or phrases can help convey emotion and create a more impactful message.

Body language and vocal delivery are critical components of an effective pitch. Proper body language techniques can help you convey confidence and establish trust with your audience. Enhancing your vocal delivery can help convey emotion and keep your audience engaged. By paying attention to these components and practicing them in your pitch, you can increase your chances of success and maximize the potential of your StartUp.

Practice Makes Perfect:

Practice is key to delivering a successful pitch. Even the most skilled public speakers and presenters spend time practicing their delivery before they step in front of an audience. Practicing your pitch allows you to refine your delivery and identify areas where you may need to improve. Here are some tips and strategies on how you can practice your pitch and make a stronger impression:

1. **Record Yourself:** One of the most effective ways to practice your pitch is to record yourself delivering it. This helps you to see and hear how you come across to others. Pay attention to your body language, tone of voice, and pacing. Find out areas where you can improve and make adjustments accordingly.

2. **Use a Mirror:** Practicing your pitch in front of a mirror can also be helpful. This allows you to see your body language and facial expressions and adjust as needed. For example, you may fidget or look down at the ground, distracting your audience. Practicing in front of a mirror can make you confident, help you become more aware of these habits, and make changes to improve your delivery.

3. **Rehearse with a Friend or Colleague**: Practicing your pitch with a friend or colleague can provide valuable feedback and help you refine your delivery. Ask your practice partner to pay attention to your body language, pace, and tone of voice and to offer constructive criticism. One effective approach is to utilize this method to pinpoint potential areas for improvement and make necessary adjustments before presenting to potential investors.

4. **Time Yourself:** Timing is an important aspect of pitch delivery. You want to ensure you deliver your pitch within the allotted time frame without rushing or going over time. Use a stopwatch or timer to time yourself as you practice your pitch. This can make you feel more comfortable with the pacing of your pitch and ensure that you deliver it within the time constraints.

5. **Practice in Different Settings:** Practicing your pitch in different settings can help you become more comfortable and confident in delivering it. For example, you may practice in a quiet room, a noisy coffee shop, or in front of friends or colleagues. Practicing in different settings can help you adapt to different environments and become more confident in your delivery.

6. **Rehearse Your Answers to Questions**: Part of delivering a successful pitch is being able to answer questions from investors. Consider the types of questions investors may ask and rehearse your answers. This can help you become more comfortable responding to questions and ensuring a clear and concise answer.

7. **Be Adaptable:** While practicing your pitch is important, it's also important to be adaptable. No two pitch opportunities are the same, and you need to adjust your delivery based on the audience, setting, or other factors. Being adaptable and able to make adjustments on the fly can help you deliver a more effective pitch and create a stronger impression on investors.

Practicing your pitch is essential for refining your delivery and making a stronger impression on investors. Recording yourself, using a mirror, rehearsing with a friend, timing yourself, practicing in different settings, rehearsing your answers to questions, and being adaptable are all effective strategies for practicing your pitch and delivering it confidently and positively. By practicing and refining your delivery, you can increase your chances of success and make a lasting impression on potential investors.

Engaging Your Audience:

Engaging your audience is a crucial part of delivering a successful pitch. Investors are likely to invest in a StartUp if they connect with the entrepreneur and are engaged in the pitch. In this subtopic, we'll explore techniques to help you engage your audience and create a connection with them.

1. **Know Your Audience:** Before you start your pitch, you must know your audience. Research the investors you'll pitch to and understand their backgrounds, interests, and investment focus. Knowing the audience will help you tailor your pitch to their interests and connect with them.

2. **Start with a Hook:** A hook is a powerful statement or question that grabs the audience's attention and draws them into your pitch. It could be a startling statistic, a personal story, or a thought-provoking question. Starting your pitch with a hook can make your presentation more memorable and engaging.

3. **Tell a Story:** Storytelling is a powerful technique for engaging an audience. Investors connect more easily with stories on an emotional level, and they can help them understand the problem you're solving and the solution you're proposing. Consider incorporating stories that showcase the real-world effects of your product or service, highlighting how it addresses your customer's specific needs and pain points.

4. **Use Visual Aids**: Slides and other visual aids can help you communicate your ideas more effectively and keep your audience engaged. Use high-resolution images and graphics to support your message and keep the design simple and easily read.

5. **Ask Questions:** A great way to engage your audience and encourage their participation is by asking questions. Ask open-ended questions that facilitate discussion and help you understand your audience's interests and concerns.

6. **Use Humor:** A touch of humor while pitching can be a powerful tool for engaging your audience and making your pitch more memorable. Use humor sparingly and keep it relevant to your message.

7. **Your Body Language:** Body language can communicate your confidence, enthusiasm, and engagement to your audience. Stand tall, make eye contact, and avoid crossing your arms or looking at the floor, as this can make you appear nervous or defensive. Use gestures to emphasize your points.

8. **Be Authentic:** Finally, be authentic to yourself in your pitch. Investors are more likely to invest in an entrepreneur who is genuine and passionate about their idea. Speak from the heart and let your enthusiasm and confidence shine through.

Engaging your audience is critical to the success of your pitch. Use these techniques to connect with your investors and keep them interested in your message. Remember to know your audience, start with a hook, tell a story, use visual aids, ask questions, use humour, use body language, and be authentic. Using these techniques, you can deliver a compelling and engaging pitch that captures the interest and investment of potential investors.

Managing Nerves and Anxiety:

Presenting your pitch to potential investors can be an intimidating experience, and it's not uncommon to feel nervous or anxious before and during your presentation. However, allowing your nerves to get the best of you can hinder your ability to deliver an effective pitch, which may negatively impact your chances of securing funding. Therefore, learning how to manage nerves and anxiety is essential. In this section, we'll explore common issues related to nerves and anxiety when presenting and provide strategies to overcome them.

One of the most common reasons for anxiety during a pitch presentation is the fear of being judged or rejected by investors. It's normal to feel nervous about presenting your StartUp idea to people who can decide whether to invest in your company. However, it's important to remember that investors are looking for great ideas and are willing to listen to entrepreneurs who can present their ideas confidently and persuasively.

To manage any fear, preparing thoroughly for your presentation is crucial. By being well-prepared and confident in your knowledge of your product or service and its market, you can increase self-confidence and reduce anxiety. Practicing your pitch with friends, colleagues, or mentors can also help you gain feedback and feel more comfortable with your presentation material.

Another way to manage anxiety during your pitch is to focus on breathing. Deep breathing exercises can help you regulate your breathing and calm your nervous system, reducing common anxiety symptoms, such as a racing heart or sweaty palms. Before you start your presentation, take a few deep breaths. Try to focus on the present moment and stop worrying about the future.

It's also essential to develop a positive mindset when presenting. Focusing on the potential positive outcomes of your pitch, such as securing funding, can help you feel more confident and motivated. Additionally, it's important to avoid negative self-talk and thoughts that may undermine your confidence. Instead, try to reframe negative thoughts into positive ones. For example, instead of thinking, "I'll never be able to persuade these investors," reframe it to "I have a great idea and am capable of presenting it convincingly."

During your pitch, it's normal to experience physical anxiety symptoms, like sweating, shaking, or dry mouth. However, remaining calm and composed is essential to deliver your pitch effectively. A technique for coping with physical symptoms is to engage in relaxation practices like progressive muscle relaxation or visualization. These techniques can help you relax your muscles and calm your mind.

Another way to manage anxiety is to focus on your audience. Stop worrying about yourself and your performance; try engaging with your audience and connecting with them. This will shift your focus from your anxiety and help you feel more comfortable during your presentation. For example, humour or personal anecdotes can help build rapport with your audience and create a more relaxed atmosphere.

Presenting your pitch to potential investors can be a nerve-wracking experience, but there are many strategies you can use to manage your nerves effectively. By focusing on your preparation, mindset, and physical symptoms, you can deliver a confident and persuasive pitch that captures the attention and interest of investors. Remember to practice, breathe deeply, and stay positive to give yourself the best chance of success.

Timing and Pace:

Timing and pace are crucial components of a successful pitch delivery. Investors are busy individuals who have to hear numerous pitches every day, so they do not have time to listen to a pitch that drags on and on. As a result, it's essential to deliver your pitch within a specific time frame and at an appropriate pace to keep your investors engaged and interested.

Understanding your pitch's allotted time is one of the first steps toward managing your timing and pace. Before presenting, make sure you know your time and plan accordingly. It's essential to remember that a pitch should be concise and to the point. If you're allotted a short period, say 5-10 minutes, make sure you can convey the essential facts of your pitch within that time frame. Similarly, if you're allotted a more extended period, say 30-45 minutes, ensure you have enough material to fill the allotted time without going overboard.

Once you know your allotted time, it's essential to structure your pitch accordingly. First, divide your pitch into logical segments, and assign time limits to each segment. For example, you could allocate two minutes for an introduction, five minutes for discussing the problem your product solves, ten minutes for discussing your solution, and three minutes for wrapping up. Sticking to your allotted time frame for each segment is important to ensure you complete your pitch on time.

In addition to managing your time, you must consider your pace when delivering your pitch. A pitch delivered too quickly can be difficult to follow, while one that's too slow can be boring. One of the best ways to maintain an appropriate pace is to practice your pitch and time yourself. For example, if you're finding that you're speaking too quickly, try to slow down by taking a deep breath before starting your pitch and consciously slowing your pace down. Similarly, if you're speaking too slowly, try to pick up the pace and inject some energy into your delivery.

Another technique for managing your pace is to use pauses effectively. Pausing can be a powerful tool to emphasize key points, create suspense, and allow your audience to absorb the information you've just presented. By inserting well-timed pauses into your pitch, you can avoid the temptation to rush through your presentation and give your audience time to catch up and follow your ideas.

Remember that not all pauses are created equal. The duration of your pause should be appropriate to the situation, and it's important not to pause for too long, as this can make your audience feel uncomfortable or lose their attention. If you're unsure about the length of your pauses, practice your pitch in front of a friend or colleague and ask them for feedback on your pacing.

Finally, it's important to be flexible regarding timing and pace. Even with careful planning, unexpected situations can arise during a pitch, and it's essential to be able to adjust your pace and timing accordingly. For example, if you're running short on time, you may need to skip over a particular section of your pitch or adjust your pace to cover all the essential points within the allotted time. Similarly, if you're running ahead of schedule, you may slow your pace to avoid finishing your pitch too early.

Timing and pace are essential to an effective pitch delivery. By understanding the allotted time for your pitch, structuring your pitch accordingly, and practicing your delivery, you can ensure that you maintain an appropriate pace and deliver your pitch within the allotted time frame. In addition, using pauses effectively and being flexible in your approach can engage your audience, emphasize key points, and increase your chances of success.

Using Visual Aids:

When it comes to delivering a pitch, visual aids can be an incredibly powerful tool. Visual aids can help to keep your audience engaged, reinforce your message, and make complex ideas more easily understood. The most common visual aids in pitches are slides, videos, and infographics.

Firstly, it's important to remember that visual aids are meant to support your message, not replace it. So your pitch should be able to stand on its own without visual aids. However, when used effectively, visual aids help you reinforce your pitch and make it more memorable.

When creating slides for your pitch, remember that less is more. Avoid information overload with too many visuals. Instead, create a few key slides that effectively communicate your message. Using images and graphics can help illustrate your points and make them more engaging.

It's also important to keep your slides simple and easy to read. Use large fonts and avoid using too much text on a single slide. The goal is to make your slides easy to understand at a glance rather than requiring your audience to read through a lot of text. Another tip is to use colour strategically. Use your brand colours to highlight key points.

When it comes to videos, they should be short and to the point. Keep your videos under 2-3 minutes, and ensure they are high quality and engaging.

Infographics can also be a powerful visual aid in your pitch, help make complex information more easily understood, and be a great way to illustrate data and statistics. When creating an infographic, please focus on the key points you want to communicate and use visuals and graphics to help illustrate them.

When using visual aids in your pitch, practicing with them beforehand is important. Make sure that you are conversant with the technology and that your slides or videos are working properly. You don't want to encounter technical difficulties during your pitch that could distract you from your message.

Finally, remember that your visual aids are meant to enhance your message, not distract from it. Therefore, use them strategically and only when they effectively communicate your message. Please don't rely on visual aids as a crutch; you must effectively communicate your message without them.

Visual aids can be a powerful tool in your pitch. When used effectively, they can keep your audience engaged, reinforce your message, and make complex ideas more easily understood. Use them strategically and keep them simple and easy to understand. With these tips, you can effectively use visual aids to enhance your pitch and increase your chances of success.

Storytelling and Humour:

When pitching a StartUp, listing facts and figures about your product or service is insufficient. To ensure a successful pitch presentation, it is essential to captivate and maintain the attention of your audience throughout the presentation. Incorporating storytelling and humour is one effective way to achieve this.

By weaving stories into your pitch, highlighting the impact of your product or service, and using humour to convey key messages, you can make your pitch more engaging and memorable. The use of storytelling and humour can also establish an intimate connection with your investors and create a more relaxed and enjoyable atmosphere. This can help build rapport and establish trust with potential investors.

Storytelling is acknowledged as a powerful tool for engaging your audience because it creates an emotional connection with your listeners. By telling a story about a real-world problem that your product or service solves, you can make your audience see the value in what you're offering. For example, if you're pitching a new app that helps people find local volunteering opportunities, you could start by telling a story about your own experience struggling to find volunteer opportunities in your community and how that led you to create the app.

When incorporating storytelling into your pitch, it's important to keep the following tips in mind:

1. **Keep it Simple:** Don't try to tell a complex story with too many details. Stick to a simple narrative that highlights the problem and solution.

2. **Make it Relatable:** Use stories your audience can relate to, showing how your product or service solves a problem your customers have experienced.

3. **Use Visuals:** Use images and other visuals to illustrate your story and make it even more engaging.

Humour is another effective tool for engaging your audience. A well-placed joke or witty remark can break up the monotony of a presentation and make it more memorable. However, it's important to use humour strategically and ensure it's appropriate for your audience.

When incorporating humour into your pitch, keep the following tips in mind:

1. **Keep it Appropriate**: Avoid offensive or controversial humor that could offend your audience.

2. **Use it Sparingly:** Don't overdo it with the jokes. Use humor strategically to break up the presentation and make it more engaging.

3. **Be Genuine:** If you're not naturally funny, don't force it. Be genuine and authentic in your delivery.

It's important to remember that while storytelling and humour can be effective tools for engaging your audience, they should not be the sole focus of your pitch. Your pitch should still focus on the value proposition of your product or service and how it solves a real-world problem. Storytelling and humour should be used to enhance your message and make it more memorable, but they should be consistent with the key points of your pitch.

Storytelling and humour are effective tools for engaging your audience and making your pitch more memorable. When incorporating these elements into your pitch, keeping them appropriate, relevant, and authentic is important. By strategically using storytelling and humour, you can create a pitch that captures your audience's attention and helps you stand out from the crowd.

Handling Questions and Objections:

Handling questions and objections from investors is an essential part of any pitch. It allows the entrepreneur to demonstrate their expertise and address investors' concerns or doubts. Here are some strategies for handling questions and objections effectively and using them as an opportunity to further engage with your audience.

1. **Anticipate Questions and Objections**: One of the most effective strategies for handling them is anticipating them in advance. This requires thorough research on the investor's background, interests, and concerns. By knowing your audience, their specific needs, and concerns, you can prepare for potential questions or objections they may have.

2. **Be Confident and Calm**: When addressing questions and objections, it's essential to remain confident and calm. Nervousness and defensiveness can undermine your credibility, and your investors may think you are hiding something. Instead, try to maintain eye contact and speak clearly, concisely, and confidently. This will

help you establish credibility and build trust with your audience.

3. **Listen Carefully:** When answering questions, it's crucial to listen carefully to the question being asked. Often, investors will have multiple questions or concerns, and it's essential to address each individually and in detail. Listen carefully to the question to understand it properly, and take a moment to clarify any doubts you may have before providing an answer.

4. **Acknowledge Concerns:** When addressing objections or concerns, it's important to acknowledge them upfront. This shows your preparedness and that you are aware of your startup's challenges. By recognizing these concerns, you can build trust with your audience and demonstrate your willingness to be transparent and honest.

5. **Evidence:** To address objections or concerns effectively, it's essential to provide evidence supporting your claims. This evidence can include customer testimonials, market research data, or financial projections. By providing concrete evidence, you can demonstrate that your startup has a solid foundation and is likely to succeed.

6. **Turn Objections into Opportunities:** One of the most effective ways to handle objections is to turn them into opportunities. For example, suppose an investor raises a concern about the competition. In that case, you can use this as an opportunity to discuss how your startup is different and why you believe you have an advantage. By addressing objections head-on, you can build credibility and show that you can think critically and adapt to new challenges.

7. **End on a Positive Note:** When addressing questions and objections, it's important to end on a positive note. Thank the investor for their question or concern, and provide a concise and compelling answer. By ending on a positive note, you can leave a lasting impression and build momentum for your pitch.

Handling questions and objections from investors is critical to any successful pitch. You can effectively handle questions and objections by anticipating potential questions and objections, maintaining a confident and calm demeanour, actively listening to concerns, acknowledging objections, providing evidence to support your claims, and turning objections into opportunities to engage further with your audience.

Perfecting your pitch delivery is crucial for securing funding and gaining the support of investors. While having a well-crafted pitch deck is necessary, focusing on delivering your message effectively is vital. By implementing the techniques and strategies discussed in this chapter, you can enhance your presentation skills, engage your audience with storytelling and humour, use visual aids effectively, manage nerves and anxiety, maintain the right pace and timing, and handle questions and objections with confidence and ease. Doing so can leave a lasting impression and increase your chances of securing funding for your StartUp.

Perfecting your pitch delivery is a challenging task, but it is necessary. By focusing on the right techniques and strategies, you can become a confident and engaging presenter, capture the attention and interest of potential investors, and ultimately succeed in achieving your Startup's goals. So, keep practicing, refining, and perfecting your pitch delivery for success.

From managing nerves and anxiety to using visual aids and storytelling effectively, each aspect of your pitch can be refined to ensure you deliver a polished and engaging presentation.

Remember, the goal of your pitch is not only to secure funding but also to inspire and connect with your audience. By using these techniques, you can create a memorable and compelling pitch that captures the attention and interest of investors, ultimately bringing your StartUp closer to success.

Chapter 5
Telling Your Story

How to Craft a Compelling Narrative

As an entrepreneur seeking investment, you have a unique story to tell. Your journey, vision, and goals all come together to create a compelling narrative that can capture the attention and interest of potential investors. In this chapter, we'll explore how you can tell your story that resonates with prospective investors and inspires them to invest in your vision.

Telling your story is a critical component of any investor pitch. It's an opportunity to showcase your vision, passion, and unique value proposition. But it's not just about sharing your journey; it's about crafting a narrative to resonate with prospective investors and inspire them to take action.

Facts Tell & Stories Sell:

"Facts tell & stories sell" is a popular saying in marketing and sales. The idea behind it is that while facts and data are important in persuading people, the stories and narratives capture their attention and emotions.

One study conducted by researchers at Carnegie Mellon University found that when people are presented with statistics and data, they tend to engage the analytical part of their brain. However, when presented with a story, they engage both the analytical and emotional parts of their brain. This can lead to a more memorable and impactful experience and a greater likelihood of persuasion.

Another study by researchers at the University of North Carolina found that stories activate areas of the brain associated with social cognition, such as empathy and understanding. This can make it easier for people to relate to and connect with the message.

Furthermore, research has also shown that stories can be more effective than data in changing people's attitudes and behaviours. For example, a study by Stanford University found that people at large were more likely to donate to a charity when they read a story about an individual in need, as opposed to when they were presented with statistics about the issue.

This is true in Pitching Too:

In the context of investor pitching, this phrase can be especially relevant. Investors are often inundated with information and data from various companies seeking funding. While having solid facts and figures to back up your business proposition is important, more is needed to capture an investor's attention and imagination.

Telling a compelling story is what can set your pitch apart from others. Your story should be clear, concise, and engaging. It should highlight the problem you're solving, the unique solution you've created, and its potential impact. A good story can help investors visualize the possibilities and see the potential in your business.

In addition, stories can be used to build credibility and trust with investors. By sharing anecdotes and personal experiences demonstrating your knowledge, expertise, and commitment, you can show investors that you're passionate about your business and have the skills and experience necessary to make it a success.

Things to Keep in Mind:

One of the most important points to remember when crafting your story is that investors seek more than just a good idea. They want to invest in a team and a vision they believe can succeed. Therefore, your story should demonstrate not only the potential of your business but also your ability to execute that potential.

While crafting your story, start by identifying the key components that will make it compelling. These include:

1. A clear understanding of your target audience
2. Your unique value proposition
3. A vision for the future of your business
4. A track record of success
5. A strong team that can execute your vision

Once you've identified these components, you can begin crafting your narrative to highlight each one. Remember the following points as well while crafting your story.

Start with a Strong Opening:

Your opening should grab your audience's attention and set the tone for the rest of your pitch. Consider starting with a personal anecdote, a startling statistic, or a thought-provoking question that will pique your audience's interest and make them eager to hear more. Igniting the audience interest is the sole purpose of storytelling.

Use Concrete Examples:

When telling your story, using concrete examples to illustrate your points is important. For example, rather than making broad statements about your business, use specific anecdotes and case studies to demonstrate your successes and showcase your potential. This will help your audience to understand better and connect with your vision.

Highlight Your Passion and Drive:

Investors want to invest in entrepreneurs who are passionate and driven. So use your story to showcase your enthusiasm for your business and your unwavering commitment to making it a success. This will help to build trust and establish a connection with your audience.

Focus on Your Unique Value Proposition:

Your story should also highlight your unique value proposition. What sets your business apart from the competition? What problem are you solving that no one else is addressing? Use your story to demonstrate your unique position in the market and why your solution is the best one for your target customers.

Address Potential Concerns:

Investors will have concerns and questions about your business, and it's important to address this head-on in your story. Be transparent about potential challenges or roadblocks, and explain how to overcome them. This will help to build trust and establish your credibility with your audience.

Use Emotion to Connect With Your Audience:

Feel free to use emotion to connect with your audience.

Investors are people, and they respond to stories that resonate with them on a personal level. So use your story to showcase your humanity and connect with your audience on a deeper level.

Telling your story is an essential part of any investor pitch. By starting with a strong opening, using concrete examples, highlighting your passion and drive, focusing on your unique value proposition, addressing potential concerns, and using emotion to connect with your audience, you can create a story that captures the attention and interest of potential investors and inspires them to invest in your vision.

Chapter 6
Developing a Unique Value Proposition

Defining Your Competitive Advantage

In the business world, having a good product or service is not enough. It would be best to communicate your USP that sets you apart from the competition and why customers should choose you over others. This is where developing a unique value proposition comes in.

Your unique value proposition is the statement that summarizes what makes your business unique and valuable. The elevator pitch explains why investors should invest in your company and why customers should prefer your product or service over others. Defining your competitive advantage is critical to the success of your business and can make all the difference in securing investment.

Steps to Develop a Unique Value Proposition:

Identify your Target Market:

The first step in developing a unique value proposition is identifying your target market. Who are the customers that you are trying to reach? What are their needs, challenges, and pain points? Understanding your target market is essential for developing a value proposition that resonates with them.

For example, if your target market is busy professionals, your value proposition might focus on saving them time and making their lives easier. On the other hand, if your target market is environmentally conscious consumers, your value proposition might focus on sustainability and reducing their carbon footprint.

Having identified your target audience and understanding their pain points and needs, develop a unique value proposition that sets you above your competitors. Your value proposition is a promise to deliver a specific benefit to your customers and makes your StartUp unique and valuable in the eyes of your potential investors.

To develop a strong value proposition, start by defining your competitive advantage. This sets your StartUp apart from the competition and gives you an edge in the market. Start by asking yourself the following questions:

1. What unique features or benefits does your product or service offer?
2. What problems does your product or service solve for your customers?
3. What sets you apart from your competitors?

Having answered these questions, you can begin to craft your value proposition.

Define your Product or Service:

After identifying your target market, you must clearly define your product or service. What does it do? How is it unique?

How does it solve the problems or meet the needs of your target market?

For example, if you are selling a new type of software, your value proposition might be that it is faster and more user-friendly than existing software. On the other hand, suppose you are selling a new eco-friendly cleaning product. In that case, your value proposition might be that it is better for the environment than and just as effective as traditional cleaning products.

Identify your Key Benefits:

Once you have defined your product or service, you need to identify its key benefits to your target market. What are the features that make your product or service stand out? How do these features benefit your customers?

For example, if your software is faster and more user-friendly than existing software, it might save users time and reduce frustration. If your eco-friendly cleaning product is just as effective as traditional cleaning products, the benefits might be that it is better for the environment and safer for families.

What's your unique selling proposition: Your unique selling proposition is the statement that summarizes what sets your business apart from others in the market. What makes your product or service unique and valuable? How does it provide a better solution than your competitors?

For example, suppose your software is faster and more user-friendly than existing software. Your unique selling proposition might be that it increases productivity and reduces the user learning curve. On the other hand, if your eco-friendly cleaning product is just as effective as traditional cleaning products, your unique selling proposition might be that it is safer for families and better for the environment.

Test your Value Proposition:

Once you have developed your value proposition, testing it with your target market is important. Do they understand it? Do they find it compelling? Does it differentiate your product or service from your competitors?

You can test your value proposition by conducting market research, focus groups, or surveys.

You can also test it by presenting it to potential investors or customers and getting feedback.

Develop a strong value proposition:

Focus on Your Customer's Needs:

Your value proposition should focus on the benefits your customers will receive. You need to understand their needs and pain points and craft your value proposition around them.

Be clear and concise:
Your value proposition should be easily understood and communicated. Avoid using technical language that may be confusing to your audience.

Highlight Your Unique Features:

Your value proposition should highlight your product or service's unique features or benefits. This is what sets you apart from your competitors.

Use Testimonials:

Using testimonials from satisfied customers is a powerful way to demonstrate the USP and value of your product or service.

Keep it Simple:

Your value proposition should be short and sweet. A simple statement communicating the benefits of your product or service can be more effective than a long explanation.

Developing a unique value proposition is essential for a successful investor pitch and a thriving business. It involves identifying your target market, defining your product or service, identifying your key benefits, and developing a unique selling proposition that sets your business apart. By testing your value proposition with your target market, you can refine your message and increase your chances of success

Chapter 7
Understanding the Market

Research and Analysis Strategies

Entrepreneurs looking to get investment from investors must understand the market well. To pitch to investors successfully, you must understand the market and its trends. Your pitch will be more persuasive if you have more information about the market. This chapter will discuss research and analysis strategies to understand the market better.

Conduct Market Research:

Market research involves gathering information about your market. This includes customer preferences, needs, industry trends, and competitor's offerings. You can conduct market research in many ways, including focus groups, surveys, and customer interviews. Market research will help you identify gaps in the market, customer needs, and opportunities you can use in your pitch.

The first step in market research is defining your target audience. Who are your ideal customers? What are their pain points and needs? Having identified your target audience, you may create questionnaires or surveys to collect data about their preferences and behaviours. You can distribute surveys online, by email, or in person. Questions must be simple and understandable to get accurate results.

Focus groups are great for gathering information about customer preferences and behaviour. Focus groups are usually small groups of people who discuss a topic or product and collect qualitative data about consumer attitudes, behaviour, and opinions toward products or services. Then, use this data to identify the key selling points and areas that need improvement.

Insight into customer preferences and behaviour is through customer interviews. Interviews with potential or existing customers can give valuable insight into what your customers' value the most about your product/service and how you can improve it.

Analyse your Competition:

This is crucial for creating a unique value proposition and establishing yourself as a leader in your industry. Studying your competition's strengths and weaknesses, pricing strategies, marketing strategies, and other tactics is important. With this information, you can identify the areas where you can stand out and make the best choice.

Begin by identifying your top competitors. Next, find companies offering similar products and services to yours, and evaluate their strengths and weaknesses. Finally, compare their pricing strategies to yours.

1. Is it more expensive or cheaper?
2. What is their market position?
3. Are they able to offer unique services or features?

SWOT Analysis:

A SWOT analysis is another useful strategy. This reviews your company's strengths, weaknesses, opportunities, threats, and threats. First, identify your strengths and weaknesses to determine how to stand out. Then, you can identify opportunities and threats and adapt your pitch to meet them.

Keep an eye on Industry Trends. Stay current with industry trends to anticipate changes in the market. This includes staying on top of new technologies, consumer behaviour changes, and shifts that occur in market demand. You can position your product/service as a solution for emerging market needs by staying informed.

Begin by looking for thought leaders and publications in your industry. You can follow them on social media or subscribe to their newsletters for recent trends and innovations. Attending industry events and conferences and keeping yourself updated on the latest industry trends can help you network with professionals in your field.

Regular environmental scans are also necessary. This includes analysing external factors that could affect your business, such as economic trends or changes in government regulations.

Data Analytics:

Data analytics tools can provide insights into customer preferences and behaviour and the performance of your business. This data can be used to identify specific areas of improvement in your pitch.

Begin by identifying the most important metrics for your business. These could be customer satisfaction scores, customer acquisition costs, churn rate, and customer acquisition costs. These metrics can then be tracked and analysed using data analytics tools.

Google Analytics, one of the most popular and widely used data analytics tools, can give you information about your website traffic, such as where visitors are coming in, how long they stay on it, and what pages they most frequently visit. In addition, SEMrush and Ahrefs can help analyse search engine optimization performance (SEO) and to identify potential opportunities to increase your website's visibility within search results.

Hootsuite and Sprout Social or similar Social media analytic tools allow you to track engagement and identify trends in the behaviour of your followers. In addition, Mailchimp and Constant Contact provide valuable insight into your email campaigns. This includes open rates, click-through rates, conversion rates, and information about the quality of your emails.

You can use data analytics tools to monitor your performance. However, they can also be used to do market research and analysis. SurveyMonkey and Qualtrics allow you to create and distribute surveys that collect feedback from potential customers. Analyse the trends in your industry and to identify potential opportunities to stand out from your competition, you can use Buzzsumo or Google Trends.

You can create a better investor pitch using data analytics tools that provide insights about your company and the market. This will allow you to draw on real-world feedback and build a solid foundation for your data. This will help you gain credibility and understand the market and your business.

Identify Trends:

Trends are patterns that develop over time. They can give valuable insight into the market's direction. Analysing trends can help you to understand your customers and the activities of your competitors. This information can be used to identify new opportunities and adapt your strategy accordingly.

Data analysis tools such as Google Trends can help you identify trends. For example, they show you how search volumes have changed over time for certain keywords. This will give you an insight into what people are looking for and how their needs and interests are changing. Social media monitoring is another useful tool that can be used to track conversations and identify emerging trends.

It is crucial to analyse the trend, once you have identified, it will help you understand the implications for your business. Ask yourself these questions:

1. What's driving this trend?
2. What is the likelihood that it will last?
3. What will this mean for your customers and competition?
4. It presents both opportunities and risks.

These questions will help you create a strategy to capitalize on the trend and respond effectively.

Evaluate Competition:

Understanding the market requires you to analyse your competitors. Therefore, it is important to understand your market and who your competitors are.

Conducting a competitive analysis is a good way to evaluate your competitors. This includes identifying your competitors and analysing their strengths, weaknesses, and opportunities. It is also important to evaluate their products and services, pricing strategies, marketing campaigns, and customer base.

You can find areas where you can stand out and get a competitive edge by conducting a thorough competitor analysis. For example, you might discover that your competitors do not meet the needs of certain market segments. This allows you to target those markets with a unique value proposition.

Identify Customer Needs and Preferences:

Understanding your customers' preferences and needs is key to success in any market. This includes gathering information about your customers, such as their demographics, buying habits, and behaviours.

Market research is a great way to get this information. You can use focus groups, surveys, or other methods to gather data from your target customer. In addition, data analysis tools such as CRM software can be used to gain insights into customer preferences and behaviour.

Once you have collected this information, you can create a customer profile. The profile should include age, gender, income, and purchasing habits. You can use this profile to tailor your sales and marketing efforts to meet the needs of your target customer.

A winning pitch to investors requires a thorough understanding of the market. First, you can thoroughly understand the market by conducting market research and analysis. This will allow you to identify new opportunities and adjust your strategy accordingly. Then, you can use this information to create a compelling story, establish a unique value proposition and build a memorable pitch deck for investors.

Chapter 8
Addressing Risks and Challenges

How to Mitigate Investor Concerns

Investors are often risk-averse and are looking for ways to mitigate potential losses. Therefore, entrepreneurs need to address potential risks and challenges in their investor pitch. Demonstrating that you have a plan to mitigate these risks can build trust with investors and increase the likelihood of securing funding. This chapter will discuss some strategies for addressing risks and challenges in your investor pitch.

Identify Potential Risks and Challenges:

Identifying risks and challenges in your investor pitch is the first step in addressing them. This requires thoroughly analysing your business model, market trends, and other factors that could impact your success. Some common risks and challenges that entrepreneurs face include:

1. **Market Risk:** Changes in the market could impact

demand for your product or service.

2. **Competitive Risk:** Increased competition in your market could make it harder to differentiate yourself.

3. **Technical Risk:** Issues with product development or technology could delay your launch or impact the quality of your product.

4. **Financial Risk:** Lack of funding or mismanagement of finances could impact a business's ability to grow and scale.

5. **Regulatory Risk:** Changes in regulations or legal issues could impact your ability to operate the business.

6. **Team Risk:** Team dynamics or key personnel leaving could impact your ability to execute your plan.

Develop a Plan to Mitigate Risks

Once you have identified potential risks and challenges, Develop a plan to mitigate these risks. This plan should outline specific strategies for addressing each risk or challenge and should be based on data and research. Here are some strategies for mitigating common risks:

1. **Market Risk:** Conduct market research to identify potential changes in the market and develop a plan to pivot your strategy if necessary.

2. **Competitive Risk:** Develop a unique value proposition and build a strong brand to differentiate yourself from competitors.

3. **Technical Risk:** Build a strong product development team and conduct thorough testing to ensure your product meets quality standards.

4. **Financial Risk:** Develop a realistic budget and financial

plan, and focus on building relationships with investors to secure funding and mitigate financial risks.

5. **Regulatory Risk:** Stay up-to-date with regulations and compliance requirements changes, and develop a plan to mitigate potential legal issues.

6. **Team Risk:** Build a strong team culture and focus on developing contingency plans for key personnel leaving or other team-related issues.

Incorporate Risk Mitigation Strategies into Your Investor Pitch:

As an entrepreneur seeking investment, it's important to be prepared to address potential risks and challenges your business may face. Investors want to feel confident about making a wise investment, and part of that involves knowing that the company they are investing in has identified and addressed potential risks.

Strategies for Mitigating Investor Concerns

1. **Be Transparent about Risks:** Don't try to hide potential risks or challenges from investors. Instead, be upfront and transparent about your business's risks. Investors will appreciate your honesty and trust you if you are open about potential pitfalls.

2. **Develop a Risk Management Plan:** Show investors that you have already planned to mitigate potential risks. This can include developing contingency plans for potential worst-case scenarios and a clear plan for managing risks.

3. **Demonstrate Your Team's Expertise:** Investors want to know they are investing in a team with the expertise to navigate potential risks and challenges. Highlight the experience and qualifications of your team, and

demonstrate how their expertise will help to mitigate risks.

4. **Address Regulatory and Legal Concerns:** If your business operates in a highly regulated industry or has legal matters that could impact your business, address these with investors. Show that you understand the regulatory and legal landscape and have a plan to comply with relevant laws and regulations.

5. **Highlight Market Opportunity:** Investors are often willing to take on risks if they see a significant market opportunity. Show investors the size and potential of your target market, and demonstrate how your business is well-positioned to capture a market share.

6. **Use Data to Back up Your Claims:** Investors are more likely to be swayed by data than by anecdotal evidence. Use data to demonstrate that your business is well-positioned to address potential risks and challenges.

7. **Evidence of Early Success**: If your business has already achieved some early success, highlight this with investors. Evidence of early traction can help to mitigate concerns about potential risks and challenges.

8. **Anticipate Investor Concerns:** Put yourself in the shoes of potential investors and try to anticipate their concerns. This will help address those concerns when they arise.

9. **Be Confident:** Finally, be confident in your business and your team. Show your investors that you are passionate about your business and believe in its potential for success.

By taking these steps, you can demonstrate to investors that you have a realistic and well-informed understanding of your business's risks and challenges and that you have already planned to address them. This will help to build trust with investors and increase your chances of getting funding.

Chapter 9
Defining Your Financials

Metrics and Projections

When presenting your pitch to investors, one of the most critical components is your financials. Investors want to see that you clearly understand your financial situation and have a well-thought-out plan for the future. This chapter will discuss the key financial metrics and projections you need to include in your pitch.

Financial Metrics:

The following are the most common financial metrics that investors want to see:

1. **Revenue:** This is the total amount of money your business generates from sales. Investors want to see a clear and realistic revenue projection that shows the potential for growth over time.

When it comes to revenue projections, it's important to be conservative and realistic. Never overestimate your revenue growth or make assumptions not backed up by data. Instead, focus on identifying key drivers of revenue growth and creating realistic scenarios for how those drivers will impact your revenue over time.

2. Gross Margin: After deducting the cost of goods sold, the remaining percentage of revenue is gross margin. A high gross margin indicates that your business is generating a profit.

3. **Net Income:** This is your business's profit after all expenses have been deducted. Investors want to see a clear and realistic net income projection that shows the potential for profitability over time.

4. **Cash Flow:** This is the amount of cash that flows in and out of your business. Investors want to see a clear and realistic cash flow projection that shows the potential for positive cash flow over time.

5. **Burn Rate:** This is the rate at which your business is spending cash. Investors want to see a clear and realistic burn rate projection that shows how long your business can operate before running out of cash.

Financial Projections:

Investors want to see realistic and well-researched financial projections that demonstrate your business's potential for growth and profitability. Here are some tips for developing strong financial projections:

1. **Use Realistic Assumptions:** Your financial projections should be based on realistic assumptions about revenue growth, expenses, and other key factors. Avoid making overly optimistic assumptions that data or market trends cannot support.

2. **Consider Multiple Scenarios**: Develop financial

projections based on multiple scenarios, including best-case, worst-case, and most-likely scenarios. This will help you and your investors understand your business's potential risks and opportunities.

3. **Review Historical Data**: Look at your financial data to find trends and patterns that can inform your financial projections. This can include revenue growth, expenses, and other key metrics.

4. **Seek Expert Advice:** Consider working with a financial advisor or accountant to develop your financial projections. Experts can provide valuable insights and guidance based on their expertise and experience.

5. **Update Your Projections**: Your financial projections should be updated regularly to reflect business and market conditions changes. This will help you and your investors stay informed about your business's potential risks and opportunities.

6. **Sensitivity Analysis:** Your sensitivity analysis should show how changes in key assumptions, such as revenue growth or expenses, will impact your financials. This analysis shows investors that you have considered the potential risks and challenges your business may face and have a plan to mitigate them.

7. **Be Prepared for Discussion:** Be prepared to discuss your financial projections in detail with investors. This includes being able to explain the assumptions behind your projections, any risks or challenges that could impact them, and how you plan to mitigate those risks.

Developing strong financial metrics and projections is critical to creating a winning investor pitch. Investors want to see a clear and realistic financial plan that demonstrates the potential for growth and profitability of your business. You can create a financial plan that will impress investors by using realistic assumptions, considering multiple scenarios, reviewing historical data, seeking expert advice, and continuously updating your projections.

Chapter 10
Building a Strong Team

Highlighting your leadership Capabilities

You know as an entrepreneur that having a strong team is essential for the success of your StartUp. Investors understand this and will examine your team closely to evaluate your company's potential. This chapter will discuss how to showcase your leadership skills and abilities when pitching to investors.

Highlight Your Expertise and Experience:

Investors are interested in knowing that you have the experience and expertise to manage your team and achieve your goals. When introducing yourself and the team, highlight your relevant experience. Include the resumes of your team in your pitch deck. Investors will be able to get a better understanding of each member's expertise and background by including their resumes in your pitch deck.

Talking about past achievements is another way to show your expertise and experience. Highlight any achievements that you or your team have made in the past. This will help you build credibility and demonstrate to investors that your team has a track record for success.

Highlight the Diversity of Your Team:

Investors also want to see a diverse team. Diverseness can take many forms, such as race, gender, ethnicity, or background. Teams with diverse qualities and experiences can bring new ideas and perspectives to the table, which can help solve problems and innovate.

Highlight the diversity within your team when pitching investors. This will show investors that you value diversity and are committed to creating a positive working environment. In addition, highlight any unique backgrounds or experiences your team members have.

Discuss Your Hiring Strategy:

Investors are interested in knowing you plan to grow your team and hire new talent. Talk about your hiring strategy and how you plan on retaining and recruiting top talent. You can also discuss your company culture, employee benefits, and growth opportunities.

Also, you can discuss any collaborations or partnerships you may have to aid in recruiting. This will show that you are a strong network person and actively seek out new talent.

Highlight Your Leadership Style:

Investors also want to know how you lead your team and leadership style. Therefore, your leadership style and approach are worth discussing when pitching investors. This will help you communicate your vision clearly to your team and show that your company has a clear vision.

It is also possible to discuss the challenges you've faced as a leader and how you overcame them. This will show your resilience and ability to adapt to changing situations.

Highlight your Industry Expertise:

Investors are looking for someone who thoroughly understands your market and industry. This requires staying current on industry trends and best practices and maintaining a strong network. Investors can benefit from your experience and expertise.

Discuss your Mentors and Advisors:

Your mentors and advisors can help make a StartUp a great asset. They can offer guidance, support, and valuable connections to help you succeed. Consider talking to your mentors and advisors when pitching investors.

It is also possible to discuss mentors and advisors you may have. This will help you build credibility and show industry leaders you are supported.

Share your Vision for the Company:

The management needs to have a clear vision of the company. They must also be able to communicate this vision to their team and investors. It means having a solid understanding of your customers and market and a plan to differentiate your company and make it successful. Make sure you clearly articulate your vision and strategy and show how your team supports it.

Investors recognize the importance of building a strong team for StartUp success. You can highlight your expertise, diversity, hiring strategy, and leadership style and your advisors and mentors to show the strength of your company's team and increase investor confidence.

Be sure to highlight your team's strengths and perspectives and be available to answer any questions investors might have. A strong team will allow you to confidently pitch your StartUp to investors.

Chapter 11
Conducting Due Diligence

Preparing for Investor Questions and Concerns

After crafting your investor pitch, it's essential to be prepared to address any questions or concerns that potential investors may have. Conducting due diligence is one of the critical steps in the investment process, and being well-prepared can make all the difference in securing funding.

Due diligence is the process whereby the investor investigates a potential investment opportunity to verify the accuracy of the information provided and assess the investment's risks and benefits. Investors typically conduct due diligence before making an investment decision to ensure that they have a clear understanding of the investment opportunity and to identify any warning signs or red flags that may indicate a higher level of risk.

As an entrepreneur seeking investment, it's essential to conduct your due diligence to anticipate and address potential investor concerns. Here are some key areas to focus on during the due diligence process:

1. **Financials:** Investors want to review your financial statements to ensure your business is financially stable and has a viable revenue model. Be prepared to answer questions about your revenue streams, cost structure, and projections for growth. Provide them with detailed financial statements, including income statements, balance sheets, and cash flow statements.

2. **Legal:** Investors will want to review your legal documentation, including your articles of incorporation, operating agreement, and any other legal agreements that may impact your business. It would help if you had answers to all the questions regarding any pending legal issues, potential liabilities, or intellectual property concerns.

3. **Market:** Investors always want to know that a market exists for your product or service and that your business has a competitive advantage. Be prepared to present market research and analysis that supports your claims and provides insights into your target customers.

4. **Management team:** Investors will want to know that your management team has the experience and skills to execute your business plan successfully. Be prepared to highlight the key members of your team and their relevant experience, as well as any gaps in your team that you plan to fill.

5. **Operations:** Investors will want to know that your business is operating efficiently and effectively. Be prepared to provide details on your operational processes, including manufacturing, supply chain, and distribution. Highlight any areas of operational excellence that differentiate your business from competitors.

6. **Exit strategy**: Investors will want to know that there is a clear path to exit their investment and realize a return. Be prepared to discuss potential exit strategies, including IPOs, acquisitions, or buyouts.

Preparing for due diligence requires significant time and effort, but it can pay off in the long run by increasing your chances of securing investment.

Tips for Conducting Due Diligence

1. **Research the Investors:** The first step is to research the investors you will pitch to. Look up their previous investments and try understanding their investment style and preferences. This will help you to craft your pitch to their specific needs and interests.

2. **Start early:** Begin preparing for due diligence as soon as possible. The due diligence process is a time taking process. It may take weeks or even months, necessitating that you must have plenty of time to gather and organize all the necessary information.

3. **Know Your Numbers:** Investors want detailed financial projections and data to support your business model. As such, you must clearly understand your financials and explain them in simple terms.

4. **Be Honest and Transparent:** It's important, to be honest about any potential risks or challenges your business may face. Don't try to hide or downplay these issues, as they will likely come up during due diligence anyway. Instead, be honest and transparent about mitigating these risks and overcoming challenges.

5. **Provide Supporting Documentation:** Besides financial projections, investors may want to see documentation such as customer contracts, patents, or

regulatory approvals. Keep these documents ready to share if requested.

6. **Stay Organized:** Keep all your documentation and information easily accessible. This will help you quickly address any questions or concerns during the due diligence.

7. **Anticipate questions:** Put yourself in the shoes of a potential investor and anticipate the types of questions they may ask. Then, prepare thoughtful and detailed answers demonstrating your expertise and business knowledge.

8. **Practice Your Pitch**: Practice your pitch to deliver it confidently. This will help you come across as prepared and knowledgeable, which can inspire confidence in investors.

9. **Seek Professional Help:** Consider working with professional service providers, such as an accountant or attorney, to help you prepare for due diligence. They can guide you throughout the process and help you identify and address potential concerns.

Conducting due diligence is a critical step in the investment process, and being well-prepared can make all the difference in securing funding.

Chapter 12
Navigating Valuation

Understanding Investor Expectations

As an entrepreneur seeking funding, valuing your company is one of the most important considerations. Determining the worth of a company is known as valuation, and it's a critical factor in negotiating funding terms with investors. Conversely, a misaligned valuation can make or break a deal, so it's essential to understand investor expectations when it comes to valuation.

Key Factors in Navigating Valuation

Fundamentals of Valuation:

Valuation is the process of determining the worth of a company based on various factors, including revenue, growth potential, assets, and liabilities. Several methods can be used for valuing a company, including the discounted cash flow, the market approach, and the asset-based approach.

Investors generally seek companies with high growth

potential and a clear path to profitability. When considering valuation, they'll evaluate a company's past financial performance, the strength of its management team, its competitive landscape, and the overall market opportunity.

Evaluating Investor Expectations:

Investors will typically consider a specific valuation range when considering a potential investment. However, this range can vary widely depending on the investor's goals, risk tolerance, and investment strategy. For example, early-stage investors may be willing to accept a lower valuation in exchange for a larger equity stake in the company, while later-stage investors may have more stringent valuation requirements.

As an entrepreneur, it's important to understand the expectations of your potential investors before entering into negotiations. Researching the typical valuation ranges for companies in your industry and at your stage of development can provide a starting point for these discussions.

Communicating Your Value Proposition:

A strong value proposition can help justify a higher valuation for your company. Your value proposition should clearly articulate the unique benefits and competitive advantages of your product or service and your company's growth potential.

Investors want to be sure that your company is addressing a significant market need and has a defensible position in the market. Communicating your value proposition effectively can help investors see the potential for long-term growth and profitability, which can justify a higher valuation.

Balancing Valuation and Dilution:

One key consideration when negotiating valuation is the potential to dilute existing shareholders. Dilution occurs when new investors are issued equity in the company, which can reduce the ownership percentage of existing shareholders.

While a higher valuation may be attractive, it's important to balance this against the potential for dilution. A significant dilution of existing shareholders can create resentment and mistrust, which can be detrimental to the company's long-term success.

Preparing for Negotiations:

Before entering into negotiations, it's essential to prepare thoroughly. This means understanding the key factors that are driving valuation in your industry and having a clear understanding of your own company's financial performance and growth potential.

It's also important to have a well-prepared pitch deck highlighting your company's unique strengths and competitive advantages. In addition, this deck should provide a clear financial picture of your company's performance, including revenue, expenses, and projections.

Seeking Professional Advice:

Navigating valuation can be a complex process, and seeking professional advice is often beneficial. This may include working with an investment banker or business valuation expert to help determine an appropriate valuation range.

It's also important to seek advice from legal and financial professionals to ensure that the terms of any funding agreement are fair and equitable. These professionals can help you understand the potential implications of different valuation scenarios and negotiate more effectively with potential investors.

Besides understanding the various valuation methods, it's important to consider investor expectations. For example, investors will often have a specific return on investment (ROI) in mind, which can influence their expectations for valuation.

Investors typically expect a higher ROI for early-stage companies still in the growth phase. This is because early-stage companies are inherently riskier than established businesses, and investors are taking on more risk by investing in them. As a result, early-stage companies may need to offer a higher equity stake to attract investors.

On the other hand, established companies with a proven track record of success will command a higher valuation. Investors may be more interested in investing in these companies because they have a lower risk profile and a track record of generating returns. However, even established companies must justify their valuation and demonstrate a clear plan for future growth.

When negotiating valuation with investors, it's important to be transparent and open to feedback. Investors may have different perspectives on what constitutes a fair valuation, and it's important to understand their perspectives and work together to find a mutually acceptable agreement. This can involve providing detailed financial projections, sharing market research and competitive analysis, and clearly understanding your company's strengths and weaknesses.

In addition to valuation, it's important to consider the terms of the investment. This can include factors such as the percentage of equity being offered, the amount of funding being raised, and the timeline for achieving certain milestones. By being transparent about these terms and working closely with investors, you can build trust and establish a strong partnership for future growth.

Navigating valuation is an important aspect of any investor pitch. By understanding investor expectations and being transparent and open to feedback, you can build a strong partnership with investors and set your company up for success.

Understanding investor expectations regarding valuation is critical to securing funding for your company. You can justify a valuation by evaluating your company's financial performance, growth potential, and competitive landscape and communicating your value proposition effectively.

Chapter 13
Exploring Different Types of Investment

From Seed Funding to IPOs

As an entrepreneur, securing funding is critical to turning your vision into a reality. However, raising capital can be daunting, particularly if you are new to the game. In this chapter, we will explore the different types of investment available to StartUps and how each can help you grow your business.

1. **Seed Funding:** Seed funding is the early-stage funding that a StartUp can receive. It typically involves small amounts of money from friends and family or angel investors to help entrepreneurs start their businesses. Seed funding can be used for product development, market research, and other essential activities. This type of funding often comes in the form of equity, which means that investors take a share of ownership in the company in exchange for their investment.

2. **Angel Investors:** Angel investors are generally wealthy individuals who invest in StartUps in exchange for a portion of the equity in the company. They typically invest in early-stage companies which still not ready for venture capital investment. Angel investors often bring valuable industry experience and connections in addition to their financial contributions. They can help StartUps with strategy, introductions to other investors, and mentoring.

3. **Venture Capital:** Venture capital (VC) is a type of funding provided by professional investors who invest in high-growth, high-potential StartUps. Venture capitalists typically invest large sums of money. This investment is also in exchange for an equity stake in the company. They are looking for StartUps with innovative ideas and a strong potential for growth. In addition to their investment, VCs often provide strategic guidance, business expertise, and access to their networks to help StartUps grow.

4. **Private Equity:** Private equity (PE) is a type of funding provided by professional investors who invest in established companies looking to expand or make a strategic acquisition. Private equity firms normally invest in companies with a proven track record of success and generate significant revenue. They invest in exchange for equity in the company and often work closely with management to help the company grow and become more profitable.

5. **Initial Public Offering (IPO)**: An initial public offering (IPO) is when a private company becomes public by selling its shares to the public for the first time. This type of funding is usually reserved for established companies that are looking to raise a significant amount of capital. Going public through an IPO allows companies to access a broader pool of investors. It can be a significant source of funding for companies looking

to expand or make strategic acquisitions.

6. **Crowd funding:** Crowd funding is a relatively new way to raise StartUp capital. It involves raising small amounts of money from a large number of people via an online platform. Crowd funding can be useful for StartUps to validate their product and gain traction with potential customers. In exchange for their investment, backers often receive a reward, such as early access to the product or a discount.

7. **Grants:** Grants are funding that does not need to be repaid. They are typically awarded by government agencies, foundations, and other organizations that support specific causes or industries. StartUps can apply for grants to fund research and development, prototype development, or other activities related to their business. Grants can be a useful way for StartUps to get initial funding without taking on debt or giving up equity.

8. **Incubators and Accelerators:** Incubators and accelerators are programs designed to help StartUps grow and succeed. They typically provide StartUps with funding and mentorship. StartUps also get access to resources such as office space, legal services, and marketing support from incubators & accelerators. In exchange for these resources, incubators, and accelerators often take an equity stake in the company.

Incubators and accelerators are programs designed to support StartUps and early-stage companies. These programs provide various resources and support services to help these companies grow and succeed.

Incubators are typically focused on helping early-stage StartUps get off the ground. They often provide office space, access to mentors and advisors, and legal and accounting support resources. Incubators can also provide access to funding, either through their investment funds or by connecting StartUps with potential investors.

On the other hand, accelerators are designed to help StartUps that are further developing. These programs are typically shorter in duration and more intensive than incubators. Accelerators provide StartUps with mentorship, guidance, and resources to help them grow quickly and achieve their goals. This can include access to funding, connections with potential partners and customers, and help with product development and market validation.

Both incubators and accelerators can be valuable resources for StartUps and early-stage companies. They provide access to expertise, resources, and funding that can be difficult to obtain independently. By participating in these programs, StartUps can increase their chances of success and accelerate their growth.

9. **Debt Financing:** Debt financing is an investment in which a company borrows money from a lender, typically a bank or other financial institution. The company agrees to pay back the principal amount plus interest over a specified time in exchange for the loan. This type of financing can be particularly attractive for companies that do not want to dilute their ownership or control.

There are two main types of debt financing: secured and unsecured. Secured debt is backed by collateral, typically an asset the borrower owns, such as real estate or equipment. On the other hand, unsecured debt is not backed by collateral and is typically issued based on the borrower's creditworthiness.

Debt financing can also be in the form of bonds, essentially loans from investors to companies or governments. Bonds typically offer fixed interest rates and have a specified maturity date, at which point the principal amount is paid back to the investor.

While debt financing can be less risky for investors than equity financing, as they have a greater degree of security with the collateral, it can also be riskier for companies as they are obligated to make regular payments and maintain a certain level of financial stability. Additionally, too much debt can negatively impact a company's credit rating and make it difficult to secure future financing.

Debt financing can be a great option for companies with steady cash flow and looking to fund specific projects or initiatives. It involves borrowing money from lenders as a debt. The debt is to be paid back with interest over a set time. This type of financing can come from banks, credit unions, or other financial institutions and can be secured (backed by collateral) or unsecured (not backed by collateral).

Convertible notes (Bonds) are a type of debt financing that can convert to equity later. They are loans that can be converted into stock when conditions are met, such as reaching a certain funding goal or at a predetermined time. Convertible notes can be a good option for early-stage companies that need to be ready to set a valuation but still need to raise capital.

Equity financing, on the other hand, means diluting ownership shares in the company to investors in exchange for funding. This type of financing can come from angel investors, venture capitalists, or even the public through an initial public offering (IPO). Equity financing can provide a larger amount of capital than debt financing, but it also means giving up a part of ownership and control of the company.

Angel investors are typically (HNIs) high net worth individuals who invest their money in early-stage StartUps. They may provide seed funding to help get a company off the ground or invest in later rounds of funding as a company grows. In addition, Angel investors are often interested in supporting innovative ideas and entrepreneurs and may provide mentorship and guidance in addition to funding.

Venture capitalists (VCs) are professional investors who manage funds dedicated to investing in high-growth companies with the potential for significant returns. They typically invest in later-stage companies that have already proven their concept and have a solid growth trajectory. VCs may provide larger amounts of funding than angel investors, but they also have stricter requirements and expectations for returns on their investment.

Finally, taking a company public through an initial public offering (IPO) involves selling ownership shares to the public for the first time. This can provide a large infusion of capital, but it also means complying with strict regulatory requirements and giving up a significant amount of control and ownership of the company.

Understanding the different types of investment available can help companies make informed decisions about their funding strategy. It is important to consider the company's current financial situation, growth potential, and long-term goals when determining which type of investment best fits. Working with experienced advisors and legal professionals can also help ensure the investment process is executed effectively and compliantly.

Chapter 14
Identifying the Right Timing

Knowing When to Seek Funding

Timing is one of the most crucial aspects of securing your business's funding. Knowing when to seek funding is as important as knowing how to pursue it. If you seek funding too early, you may have a clear direction or vision for your business, making it easier to convince investors to invest. Conversely, if you seek funding too late, you may miss opportunities to grow your business and stay ahead of your competitors.

In this chapter, we will explore the key factors to consider when identifying the right timing for seeking funding, including the stage of your business, growth trajectory, market conditions, and investor sentiment. We will also discuss the potential risks and benefits of seeking funding at different stages of your business and the different types of investors you may encounter along the way.

Stages of Business:

The stage of your business is crucial to consider when identifying the right timing for seeking funding. For example, StartUps may need funding much earlier in their growth trajectory than established businesses. Typically, StartUps seek funding during the early stages of their development, often called the seed or pre-seed stages.

At this stage, the company validates its business idea, builds its team, and develops its product or service. Seed funding is often used to cover the costs of market research, product development, and other early-stage expenses. Seed funding usually comes from angel investors, venture capital firms, and incubators or accelerators.

Once a StartUp has successfully validated its business idea and developed a working prototype or minimum viable product (MVP), it may be ready to move on to the next growth stage: the StartUp stage. At this point, the company may generate revenue, build its customer base, and scale its operations. StartUp funding is typically used to fuel growth and expansion and may include additional rounds of seed funding and early-stage venture capital.

As the business grows and matures, it may enter the growth stage, seeking additional funding to support its continued expansion. At this stage, the company may have a proven track record of success, a well-established customer base, and a clear path to profitability. Growth-stage funding may include later-stage venture capital, private equity, or debt financing.

Market Conditions:

Market conditions are another critical factor when identifying the right timing for seeking funding. In a strong market, investors are more willing to invest in StartUps and other high-growth businesses as they see more potential for a significant return. In a weaker market, however, investors may be more risk-averse and less likely to invest in StartUps or other high-risk ventures.

Please remember that market conditions may change rapidly, and what may be a favourable investment climate today may not be tomorrow. As such, it is crucial to monitor market conditions closely and be prepared to adjust your funding strategy accordingly.

Investor Sentiment:

Investor sentiment is another critical factor when identifying the right timing for seeking funding. Economic conditions, political events, and industry trends can influence investor sentiment.

Investors who are bullish on a particular industry or technology may be more likely to invest in StartUps and other high-growth businesses operating in that space. Conversely, investors who are bearish on a particular industry or technology may be less likely to invest in StartUps operating in that space.

Another point to remember is that investor sentiment can be fickle and change rapidly. As such, it is crucial to stay up-to-date on industry trends and be prepared to adjust your funding strategy accordingly.

Competition:

When considering when to seek funding, it's important to evaluate the level of competition in your industry or market. Securing funding may take more work if many other companies offer similar products or services. Investors are likely to be more cautious about investing in a crowded market, as the risk of failure is higher when many companies compete for the same customers.

On the other hand, if your company is operating in a relatively untapped market or has a unique product or service that sets you apart from the competition, you may be more attractive to investors. In such cases, it may be easier to secure funding, and you may have more negotiating power when it comes to terms and valuations.

It's also important to consider the potential impact of new or emerging competition. For example, there are indications that new competitors may enter the market soon. In that case, it may be wise to seek funding sooner rather than later to establish a stronger foothold and stay ahead of the competition. On the other hand, if there are no immediate threats from new competitors, it may be beneficial to seek funding once your company has achieved certain milestones or achieved greater traction in the market.

Understanding the competitive landscape of your industry or market is important when identifying the right timing to seek funding. In addition, it can help you determine whether it's the right time to pursue funding or focus on building your business further before seeking investment.

Business Goals:

Your business goals and objectives should also guide when to seek funding. For example, seeking funds at the earliest may be necessary to scale your business quickly. On the other hand, if your goal is to maintain a steady pace of growth and profitability, seeking funding may not be as urgent.

The company must have clear and achievable business goals before seeking funding, as this will help determine the amount and type of funding needed and the timing of the funding. For example, if a company's goal is to launch a new product, it may require a significant amount of funding upfront to cover research and development costs. In contrast, if the goal is to expand into a new market, the funding may focus more on marketing and sales efforts.

Having clear business goals also helps to demonstrate to potential investors that the company has a solid plan for growth and profitability. In addition, investors want to see that the company has a clear vision for how the funding will achieve specific goals and generate returns.

Cash Flow:

Cash flow is a critical factor in determining when to seek funding. If your business generates enough cash flow to sustain operations and invest in growth, seeking funding may be optional. However, if your cash flow is tight and limiting your growth potential, seeking funding may be the only way to expand your operations.

When a business seeks funding, it is important to clearly understand its current and projected cash flow. Investors will want to know how much money the company is generating, how much it is spending, and how much it will need to achieve its goals.

A solid cash flow management plan is essential when seeking funding. This includes monitoring cash flow, understanding the timing of inflows and outflows, and ensuring the StartUp has enough cash to cover its expenses and investment needs.

In addition, having a positive cash flow can make a business more attractive to investors, as it demonstrates the ability to generate revenue and manage expenses effectively. A positive cash flow can also give a business more flexibility regarding funding, as it may be able to delay seeking funding until it is in a stronger financial position.

Building a Strong Team:

Building a strong team means having a team in place that is capable of executing the company's business plan and achieving its goals. Investors are not just investing in the product or service but also in the people behind it. Therefore, having a strong team is crucial in attracting funding.

A strong team consists of individuals with the necessary skills and expertise to execute the business plan effectively. The team should clearly understand the company's goals and objectives and have a shared vision of where the company is headed. In addition, investors want to see that the team has a track record of success and a plan for future growth.

Building a strong team also involves having a strong leadership structure in place. The CEO and other key executives should understand their roles and responsibilities clearly and be able to communicate the company's vision and strategy to investors effectively. In addition, having a diverse team that brings different perspectives and skills to the table is important, which can help mitigate risk and lead to better decision-making.

Investors will also look at how the team is compensated and incentivized. They want to see that the team is aligned with the company's goals and that they are motivated to work towards its success. This can include equity ownership or other performance-based incentives.

Building a strong team is critical in determining the right timing to seek funding. A strong team with the necessary skills and expertise can help mitigate risk and increase the likelihood of success, which is important to investors. It's important to clearly define each team member's roles and responsibilities and plan for future growth. Additionally, having a diverse team with different perspectives can lead to better decision-making and a higher chance of success.

Identifying the right time to seek funding is essential for the success of any StartUp. You need to understand your business needs, assess your financial situation, evaluate market conditions, identify growth opportunities, build a strong team, develop a fundraising strategy, and plan for the future. Doing so lets you determine the right time to seek funding and secure the resources required to achieve your goals.

Chapter 15
Building an Investor Pipeline

Strategies to Build Relationships and Networks

A strong investor network is crucial for any business looking to raise capital. Entrepreneurs must build relationships with investors who share their vision and are open to financial support to secure investment. It can be difficult, but it is possible with the right strategies.

Strategies for Developing an Investor Pipeline

Get started early:

Start early to build a pipeline of investors. Start networking as soon as possible with potential investors. Entrepreneurs can network with potential investors by participating in StartUp competitions and attending industry events.

Entrepreneurs can build trust and establish relationships

with investors by starting early. This is especially important when looking for funding in the future. Investors prefer to invest in businesses they trust.

Prioritize Quality over Quantity:

It is important to emphasize quality when building an investor pipeline. Entrepreneurs must identify potential right investors for their business and then build relationships with them. This involves researching potential investors and understanding their investment criteria.

Investors who are good for business are more likely than others to invest. Therefore, it is better to build relationships with investors interested in the business than with many who might not be.

Use Existing Relationships:

To build their investor network, entrepreneurs should use existing relationships. Reach out to family, friends, and professionals interested in investing in your business.

Entrepreneurs should also look for partnerships with other businesses or organizations with access to investors. Entrepreneurs can also work with incubators, accelerators, or other support organizations to meet potential investors.

Create a Strong Online Presence:

A strong online presence is necessary for any business looking to raise funds in today's digital world. Entrepreneurs should create a professional website highlighting their businesses and providing information for potential investors.

Social media can help you build relationships with potential investors. You can connect with potential investors through platforms like AngelList, Twitter, or LinkedIn. To stay in the forefront of your mind, share updates on your company's progress with investors and engage with posts by them. Refrain from being pushy or aggressive with your outreach and focus on making genuine connections and adding value.

Participate in Pitch Events:

Participating in pitch events is a great way of building investor relationships. Pitch events allow entrepreneurs to present their businesses and meet potential investors.

Entrepreneurs must prepare a compelling pitch and practice their presentation skills before going live. This includes telling a compelling story and highlighting the business's unique value proposition.

Keep in Touch:

It's crucial to keep in touch with potential investors once entrepreneurs have built relationships. This means sharing information and updates regularly about the business.

Entrepreneurs can maintain contact with potential investors to keep them interested and engaged in their business. This is a great way to get funding. Investors always invest in businesses that they know.

Get Referrals:

Ask your industry contacts and mentors for referrals to potential investors if you have a strong network. Cold outreach is less effective than referrals from trusted sources because the investor is more likely to trust to be referred by someone they are familiar with. Referrals from trusted sources can be more effective than cold outreach. Follow up promptly and thank the person who introduced you.

Build Reputation:

A strong reputation is one of the best investor pipeline strategies. You can do this by establishing a track record for success, being recognized as an innovator or thought leader, and creating a positive company culture. Investors look for companies with a strong team and a clear view of the future. As a result, you can build trustworthiness and innovation in your company and attract potential investors.

Building an investor pipeline requires effort, time, and a strategic approach. You can attract potential investors by focusing on networking and building relationships. This will position your company to succeed. Always be kind, respectful, and genuine. It would be best if you did not focus on short-term gains. These strategies will allow you to build a strong investor network supporting your company's growth and success.

Chapter 16
Building Your Pitch Roadmap

Structuring Your Pitch for Maximum Impact

Delivering a compelling pitch to investors in today's highly competitive business environment is crucial. Your pitch is vital to your chances of getting investment, whether seeking seed capital or going public. Investors are interested in more than a great idea or a well-constructed business plan.

Your pitch should be crafted in a way that appeals to potential investors. It should highlight the strengths of your company. A pitch roadmap is a useful tool. A pitch roadmap is a strategy framework that organizes and presents your pitch to maximize its effectiveness and persuasiveness.

This chapter will discuss the essential elements of a pitch plan and offer practical strategies to help you create a winning pitch. We will discuss the steps required to make a pitch stand out, from identifying your target audience to creating a compelling story. Whether you're a StartUp founder or an established business leader, we will show you how to structure your pitch to make it stand out.

Importance and Usefulness of a Pitch Roadmap:

A pitch roadmap is essential to creating a compelling investor pitch. A pitch roadmap is a strategic plan outlining your pitch's key elements. It includes the structure, messaging, and flow. It's a guide to help entrepreneurs organize their ideas and communicate their vision effectively to potential investors.

A pitch roadmap serves two purposes: it gives investors a concise overview of your company. It highlights the key competitive advantages that make you stand out from other companies in this market. This serves as a guideline for your pitch. It helps you keep your message focused and avoids the temptation to go off-topic.

Your target investors should have a well-crafted pitch roadmap tailored to their needs. The pitch roadmap should be easy to understand and follow. It should have a clear introduction that grabs investors' attention, followed by a compelling body explaining your business case and concluding with a strong, lasting impression. Finally, an investor can ask potential questions or raise objections to the pitch roadmap, which helps entrepreneurs prepare for them.

A pitch roadmap is a vital tool for entrepreneurs looking to raise capital. You can improve your chances of getting funding and take your business to the next level by creating a strategic plan for your pitch.

Setting Goals and Objectives for the Pitch:

Defining your goals and objectives is a key step in creating a winning pitch structure. Your pitch should be clear and aligned with your business goals. This requires you to take the time to consider what your pitch should accomplish and what message you wish to convey to your audience.

A pitch can have three main goals: raising capital, securing partners, and gaining market traction. It doesn't matter what your goals are; it is important to define them and ensure they are achievable and realistic clearly. This will allow you to target your audience and focus your message.

When defining your goals, looking at the context of your industry and business is important. What are the major trends and challenges in your market? What is your unique contribution to this market? These questions will help you better understand the bigger picture and position your pitch to resonate with potential partners or investors.

Setting yourself up for success by defining your goals is the ultimate goal. You can make a plan to guide you toward your goals and help you communicate effectively with your audience by being clear about your objectives and why.

Key Points to Include In Your Pitch:

It is crucial to identify key points that investors should be able to see in your pitch. These key points should highlight the most important aspects of your business and demonstrate why it is worth investing in.

A problem-solution framework is one way to approach this. It defines the problem that your company is trying to solve and the solution you have for it. This is a great way to attract investors and show your knowledge of the market and customer requirements.

Your unique value proposition (UVP) is another important point. This is your business' essence and what makes it stand out. This should communicate the value of your product or service and explain how it is better than other solutions on the market.

The pitch should also include information about your team's experience and capabilities, the leadership team, and any advisors. Investors can use this information to assess the quality and ability of the team to implement the business plan.

It would help if you also discussed the market's size and potential growth, the competitive landscape, your strategy to overcome obstacles to entry, financial projections, metrics, and any strategic alliances or collaborations supporting your business plan.

The key points that you include should tell a compelling story about your business and its investment potential. As a result, you can increase your chances of success in attracting investors and funding.

Compelling Opening Statement:

Creating a compelling opening statement is crucial to grab investors' attention and set the tone for all subsequent pitches. Therefore, your opening statement should convey your company's value proposition clearly and concisely and spark investor interest.

You must get to know your audience to create an engaging opening statement. Then tailor your message to the investor's needs. Ask yourself the following question: What is the most pressing problem your company solves? What makes your solution different and better than the rest? What will your solution do to create value for investors and their portfolios?

Once you clearly understand your value proposition and target audience, it is time to start writing your opening statement. Remember that your opening statement should be, at the most, 30 seconds long and must be memorable and grab attention.

How to Create a Memorable Opening Statement:

1. **Start with a Hook:** To grab investors' attention, you need to start with a hook.

2. **Define the problem**: State the problem you are solving and its impact on your market.

3. **Your solution:** Present your solution and explain why it is the best.

4. **Highlight the benefits:** Highlight your key benefits and explain how they add value to the investor's portfolio.

5. **Create a call for action:** After your opening statement, create a call for action that encourages investors to listen to your pitch.

The opening statement is your opportunity to make a first impression and set the tone for the rest. So make sure to write a memorable and compelling opening statement that highlights your unique business value proposition.

Creating a Clear Value Proposition:

A clearly defined value proposition is the starting point of a solid pitch roadmap. A value proposition is a short statement summarising your product or service's unique benefits to clients or customers. This makes your company stand out from the rest and shows investors why you can succeed in the market.

You must first understand your target market to develop a value proposition. What problem can your product or service solve? What unique benefits does it offer that other solutions in the market don't? These questions will enable you to identify the key features or benefits you should highlight in your pitch.

Once you have identified your unique value proposition, you must communicate it. It should be simple to comprehend and easily remembered. Then, it would help if you tailored it to your audience. What is most important for your investors? What are their goals? Understanding your audience will help ensure your value proposition is appealing to them and meets their needs.

Clearly communicating your value proposition clearly and showing how your product/service will generate revenue is crucial. Investors also need to see the value. You can discuss your business model, revenue streams, and potential growth. Investor confidence can be increased by providing data and projections to support your claims.

To build a solid pitch roadmap, developing a clearly defined value proposition is important. This is the basis of your pitch and helps to communicate why your company is an attractive investment opportunity. In addition, you can make your pitch more appealing to investors by focusing on the unique benefits of your product or service and tailoring your message for your audience. This will help you set your business up for success.

Creating a Strong Storyline:

A compelling storyline and narrative are essential parts of a winning pitch. This helps you engage investors by giving a clear picture of your company, its goals, and how it can solve a particular problem in the market. The art of storytelling has been a key part of pitching because it creates an emotional connection between investors and the company.

While creating a compelling storyline, the first step is to identify the main themes of your pitch. These themes should be aligned with your business goals and objectives. They should also reflect the problems your product or service is trying to solve. Having identified the key themes, you can create a narrative to convey them engagingly and cohesively.

The classic three-act structure is a great way to create a compelling story. The first act introduces your business problem or opportunity. This sets the scene for your pitch by highlighting market gaps or unmet needs your product/service aims to fill. This is the final act of the story. It's where you present your solution and how it solves the problem. The second act is the most important part of your pitch. It should highlight the unique value proposition of the business. Finally, in the resolution, you summarize your pitch and make a call to action.

It is important to remember your audience when crafting a compelling storyline. Your story should be tailored to your target investors' interests and needs. Think about their investor type, their investment style, and what businesses they invest in. You can engage and persuade them to invest by tailoring your story to their interests.

Concrete and relatable examples are another important aspect of crafting a compelling storyline. Instead of focusing on abstract concepts or data, you should use real-life examples and case studies to demonstrate the impact of your company. This makes your pitch more memorable for investors and more relatable.

A compelling storyline and narrative are essential components of a winning pitch. First, you can identify key themes and use a three-act structure. Then tailor your story to your audience and use concrete examples to create a pitch that engages investors and persuades them to invest in your company.

Highlight Your Competitive Advantage:

A key aspect of creating a successful investor pitch plan is highlighting your company's competitive advantages. Investors want to see what makes your company stand out from other companies in the market. This is your competitive advantage.

It is important to do thorough market research to determine the gaps and opportunities that your company can address. This research will help you to understand your target market as well as the preferences and needs of your customers.

Once you understand your target market, you can identify your unique selling proposition (USP). Your USP makes your product or service stand out from the rest. Your USP should be concise and clear. It should sum up the company's value.

Presenting your competitive advantage clearly and concisely in your pitch is important. Investors should understand your competitive edge and be able to communicate it to them.

It will help if you highlight your USP, any patents or intellectual properties that your company has, and any strategic alliances or partnerships you have formed. These factors can help you increase your competitive advantage and your company's worth to investors.

A successful pitch roadmap will highlight your company's competitive advantage. In addition, investors will be able to understand your USP by clearly defining it and supporting it with data and evidence.

How to Address Risks and Challenges:

Every investor is aware that there are risks involved in investing. Therefore, discussing the risks and challenges your company might face in your pitch is crucial. Investors will see that you have thought through all possible roadblocks and have a plan to overcome them.

Start by identifying and analysing the main risks and challenges facing your company. These could be industry-specific risks like technological advances or regulatory changes that could impact your business or general risks like economic downturns and unexpected market shifts.

After identifying the risks and challenges, you can address them in your pitch. For example, discuss your company's risk management plans or outline how you will adapt to changing market conditions. It is important to be open about potential obstacles and show investors you have plans to overcome them.

While it is essential to address risks and challenges, you shouldn't dwell too much on them. Instead, you can use them to show your company's resilience and adaptability. Doing so will show investors that your company has a plan for the future regardless of any challenges.

It's important to identify any strengths or unique assets that your company has to help reduce these risks. For example, a strong patent portfolio can help protect your company from competitors looking to copy your products and services.

Your pitch should address risks and potential challenges. This will help you build investor trust and confidence in the company. In addition, investors will be impressed by your ability to communicate potential obstacles and outline a plan to overcome them.

Provide Evidence & Supporting Data:

A successful pitch roadmap requires you to provide evidence and support data. It is not enough to claim your company's potential; you need to provide evidence and supporting data to support your claims. This evidence could include customer testimonials, market research, financial projections, or data about your company's past successes.

Using visuals like graphs, charts, and images to support your pitch is a great way to include supporting data. Visuals are another great way to make your presentation memorable and more interesting. They also help you to communicate complex information clearly and concisely.

It is crucial to present data that is relevant and useful. This includes highlighting key trends and metrics that show the potential of your company, as well as addressing any risks or challenges that might arise.

It is important to provide evidence and data. However, it is equally important to explain the significance and relevance of this information. This involves defining the context of how the data supports your business goals and overall value proposition. This will help investors understand your business better and increase their value.

End Your Pitch with a Strong Call to Action:

Successful pitches are more than just about pitching a great idea or proving its potential. It is about convincing investors to invest in your company. Your final pitch should leave a lasting impression and inspire your audience to take the next steps.

A strong call to action can only achieve this goal. This is where you state clearly what you want your audience to do next. This could be anything from scheduling a follow-up meeting to investing in your company. It doesn't matter what it is; it should always be clear and concise.

How to Make a Compelling Call to Action:

1. **Make your Call to Action Specific:** Be clear about what you want your audience to do. You want your audience to know exactly what you're asking them to do, whether making an investment, scheduling a meeting, or taking other actions.

2. **Create Urgency:** Create urgency around your call for action. Your audience should know that time is short and must act fast to seize the opportunity.

3. **Give Incentives:** Incentivize your audience to take action. You could offer a special deal, a discount, or exclusive access to certain services or products.

4. **Demonstrate Confidence in Your Pitch:** Your audience should know that you believe in your ability to succeed and that it is smart to invest in your company.

5. **Your audience should be thanked:** Thank them for their time. Let your audience know you appreciate their opportunity to present your company.

A strong call to action is an essential element of any pitch. You can make a lasting impression and persuade your audience to take action by being clear, concise, and urgent. Always thank your audience for their attention and follow up with them after the pitch.

Chapter 17
Responding to Investor Questions

It's more than just presenting a compelling pitch to investors. It's not enough to present a great pitch to investors. You must also be ready to answer any questions that they might have about your company, finances, market, or competition. The Q&A section of the pitch is crucial and can often make or break your investment.

Investors will ask questions to understand your business better and assess the risks and potential opportunities. They also want to determine if your venture suits their investment portfolio. Therefore, preparing for and anticipating these questions as an entrepreneur is crucial to show your expertise and instilling confidence in the venture.

This chapter will discuss the art and science of Q&A. We'll also give you tips and strategies to answer investor questions effectively. You'll learn how to answer investor questions effectively, from understanding what they want to be concise and convincing in your answers.

Understanding the Purpose of Q&A:

StartUps must understand the purpose of Q&A to respond to investor questions effectively. Investors can use the Q&A session to get additional information, clarify their doubts or concern, and evaluate the credibility of the business proposition.

The Q&A session is also a chance for investors to assess the entrepreneur's communication skills, knowledge, and ability to answer difficult questions. In addition, this is a chance for entrepreneurs to show their expertise and passion for their business. It also allows them to showcase their ability to think independently.

Remembering that Q&A sessions are not about answering investors' questions is important. It's about building trust with investors and showing them that the StartUp is willing to work together with the investors toward a common goal. Entrepreneurs must approach the Q&A with a strategic mind-set. They should use the opportunity to highlight their strengths and address any weaknesses in their pitch.

Common Questions:

Preparing for investor Q&A sessions is a crucial part of your preparation. This involves identifying the questions investors might ask and developing concise and thoughtful responses to address their concerns.

It is important to imagine yourself as an investor to anticipate common questions. Think about what information they might need before investing in your company. These questions could include your market and competition, team, and growth plans.

You can identify common questions by researching the

questions entrepreneurs in your industry were asked at investor presentations and pitch events. Then, you can draw from your past Q&A sessions to anticipate the questions you will be asked.

You can anticipate common questions and prepare well-crafted answers showing your business knowledge. Investors may also have concerns or objections. To feel confident, the StartUp must expect common questions and be prepared to answer them. This will help you relieve any anxiety about the Q&A session.

Framing Your Responses:

It's not about what you say but how you say it. Therefore, it is important to respond to investor questions concisely and directly.

A simple structure is a key strategy to frame your responses. To ensure you understand the question, start by rephrasing it. Next, give a concise and direct answer. Then, add some context or elaboration that will support your answer.

When framing your responses, the language used to answer should be easy to comprehend and understand. Avoid using complex terminology or technical jargon that could confuse investors. Instead, illustrate your points using plain language, analogies, and examples.

When answering investor questions, it's important to be aware of your tone and demeanour. You should be confident and authoritative but also approachable and engage the investor. Be open to suggestions and feedback, and show genuine interest in investors' concerns.

To be able to navigate the Q&A section of an investor pitch, it is important that you frame your responses in a clear, concise, and easily understood manner. This will ensure that your responses are received well and make a good impression on potential investors.

Be Honest and Transparent:

Answering investor questions requires that you are honest and open in your answers. Investors seek transparency and openness about your business's strengths and weaknesses. In addition, investors may have tough questions about your product, market, or team.

Although ignoring potential problems or putting a positive spin on everything can be tempting, this approach can backfire. Investors are skilled and knowledgeable and can see through optimistic or evasive responses. Investors may lose faith in you and your company if they feel you aren't being honest with them.

Instead, be open and honest about any weaknesses or potential risks in your business. Then, recognize the problems and outline your plans to overcome them. This shows that you can understand your market and business and take proactive steps to reduce risks.

Maintaining a balance between honesty and confidence in your company and vision is also important. It is important to show that you are aware of possible challenges and confident in your abilities to overcome them.

Being honest and transparent with investors will build the Startup's trust and credibility and ultimately lead to a successful funding round.

Avoid Jargon, Technical Language:

Investors can come from many backgrounds and industries. While they may be well-versed in business concepts and practices and may even understand the terminology and acronyms specific to your industry, they might not know how to use them. Therefore, it is important to use simple language when answering questions.

The clear and concise language will help you ensure that investors understand your answers and are well-received. You can also avoid technical language and jargon to make yourself more approachable and relatable. This can help you build a positive relationship with potential investors.

One tip to make technical concepts more understandable is to use metaphors or analogies. For example, suppose you are in the biotech industry and need to explain complex processes. In that case, an analogy might be comparing it to a household appliance or everyday object. As a result, investors can visualize the concept more easily and understand its significance better.

You should also make sure you define acronyms and technical terms that you use. These terms can be explained as you go, or provide a glossary in your pitch materials. This ensures everyone is on the same page and helps avoid any confusion or misunderstandings arising from technical language.

Keeping Control of the Conversation:

Maintaining control over the Q&A session is important so potential investors can hear your message. Remember that Q&A is a two-way conversation. While you will answer all questions, it's crucial that you keep the conversation on track and get your main points across.

Bridging statements are a way to keep control of the conversation. These statements allow you to seamlessly transition from the question to the point you wish to make. For example, if an investor asks about potential risks in your business, you might respond with, "That's great. I'm glad that you brought it up." We have taken many steps to reduce that risk, including ..."

Closed-ended questions are another way to keep control. These questions can be answered simply with a yes or no answer and can be useful tools to steer the conversation in a particular direction.

During the Q&A session, being aware of your body language and voice tone is important. Make eye contact with the person asking your question and communicate clearly and confidently. It's easy to lose focus if you are nervous or uncertain.

Handling Difficult or Challenging Questions:

Although most questions for investors are straightforward, you may encounter challenging questions from time to time. These questions could be anything from asking about areas you'd rather not to challenging your assumptions or business model. It doesn't matter what the question is; it's important that you remain calm and composed when addressing it.

A good strategy to handle difficult questions is first to acknowledge the issue or concern being raised and then to respond thoughtfully. Don't get defensive or emotional; don't try changing the subject or deflecting the question. Instead, take time to think about the question and respond so that it demonstrates your understanding and ability to address the issue effectively. It's fine to take some time to think about how you should respond to difficult questions. However, recognizing that the question is good can help you to keep the conversation on track and to ease tension.

Remember that even difficult questions can be a chance to show your knowledge and expertise. These questions can be answered effectively, and you will build trust with investors.

Follow up with Additional Information:

Investor questions can be answered during or after a pitch by following up with additional information. Investors may have additional questions after your pitch. Investors may be concerned about your ability to provide additional information. This shows that you are proactive and ready to help.

It is crucial to respond promptly and professionally when following up with additional information. Do not make investors wait too long to get a response. This can be perceived as a lack of commitment. It is a good idea if you have a plan for how you will follow up with investors. This includes who will provide additional information and how long it takes.

The investor's specific concerns and needs should dictate the information you provide. For example, an investor may request additional data or analysis if they have questions about your financial projections. You may also provide resumes and bios for investors with questions about your team's experience.

It's crucial to find a balance when following up with investors. While you should provide sufficient information to address investor concerns, it is important not to overwhelm them with unnecessary or irrelevant information. On the other hand, it is important to follow up with investors and ensure they are satisfied with the answers.

For entrepreneurs looking to attract investors, it is crucial to master the art of Q&A. Effectively responding to questions requires strategic planning, careful preparation, and maintaining control over the conversation. Successful Q&A sessions are built on anticipating common questions, being transparent and honest, using technical language, and avoiding jargon are key elements. Additional information and follow-up can strengthen your pitch and show your commitment to forming a partnership with potential investors. These tips and strategies will help impress investors and secure funding.

Chapter 18
Attracting Investor Attention

Promoting and Marketing Your Pitch

Your ultimate goal as an entrepreneur looking for funding is to get your pitch to investors willing to consider your company. In today's highly competitive market, having a solid business idea and a compelling pitch is not enough. You must also know how to market and promote your pitch to attract potential investors.

Marketing your pitch and making cold calls to investors is not enough. It is about knowing who your target investors are, their location, and how you can best communicate your message. We will discuss the different strategies and tactics you can use to make your pitch stand out in a competitive marketplace. We'll also discuss the essential elements of a successful marketing campaign. This includes defining your target audience and crafting a compelling message, and how to leverage various marketing channels to increase your reach. This chapter has the information and techniques to get investors' attention for the desired funding.

Marketing and Promotion of Your Pitch:

It is difficult to get investor attention in today's highly competitive market. Even if you have a great idea or a compelling pitch, it won't be enough to make investors pay attention. Entrepreneurs and StartUps must invest substantial time and resources in marketing and promotion to ensure the right investors hear their pitches. Marketing and promotion can make the difference between success and failure in fundraising campaigns.

Marketing and promotion are designed to raise awareness and generate interest in the opportunities you present to investors. It's similar in many ways to other marketing campaigns, where the primary goal is to attract the attention of your target audience and compel them into action. Investor pitches should encourage them to invest in your company.

Marketing and promotion can make your pitch stand out and convince investors to invest. This can help build your brand and position your company as an industry leader. This chapter will discuss the different strategies and tactics you can use to promote and market your pitch to investors to increase your chances for funding.

Create Your Investor Outreach Strategy:

A key aspect of pitching your pitch and securing investor attention is to develop an Investor Outreach Strategy. This strategy includes reaching potential investors via various channels, including personal networks and industry events.

Identifying your target investors is the first step to developing an outreach strategy. Find potential investors interested in your company and decide the best way to reach them. It would help to consider their investment preferences, investment stage, and industry preference. This will allow you to tailor your message and approach to their needs and interests.

Once you have identified potential investors, compile a complete list of them and their contact information. This can include angel investors, venture capital firms, individuals, and other funding sources.

Next, create a communication plan to reach potential investors. The communication plan should include your messaging, timing, and frequency of communications. This plan can include emails, phone calls, and social media outreach.

It is crucial to create a compelling message that conveys your value proposition and grabs the attention of potential investors. The message should be customized for each investor and highlight the benefits of your business to their investment preferences.

To promote your pitch, you should reach out to potential investors and use your professional and personal networks. Get in touch with family members, friends, and colleagues to find potential investors. To network with potential investors, attend industry conferences, and gain exposure for your business.

You can market your pitch effectively to potential investors by creating a comprehensive outreach strategy. This will increase your chances of getting funding.

Use Social Media to Reach Investors:

Social media can also help you reach potential investors and build your brand. Social media offers a unique opportunity to connect with people and groups that may be interested in your company.

It is important to establish an online presence before you

can use social media effectively for investor outreach. This involves creating professional profiles on relevant platforms, posting regularly engaging content, and engaging with your followers.

You can promote your pitch using social media by sharing updates about your company's progress, upcoming events, and other newsworthy developments. This will keep your followers engaged and informed about your brand and attract potential investors interested in your industry.

Participating in relevant discussions and groups on social media is another strategy. This will allow you to be a thought leader within your industry and establish relationships with potential investors and professionals. You can attract potential investors by sharing your expertise and generating interest in your company.

Social media advertising can also help to reach new audiences and promote your pitch. Facebook and LinkedIn provide targeted advertising options. These platforms allow you to target individuals based on job titles and interests. You can get the attention of potential investors by creating targeted ads that highlight your unique value proposition and drive traffic to your pitch.

You can build relations with investors on social media to promote your pitch. You can increase your reach and establish yourself as an expert by effectively leveraging these platforms.

How to Craft a Catchy Email Pitch:

Email can be a powerful tool to reach potential investors and get their attention. Investors are bombarded with emails every day from entrepreneurs looking for funding. Therefore, your email pitch must be compelling and well-crafted to stand out in investors' inboxes.

A compelling email pitch starts with a concise and clear

subject line. This succinctly summarizes the purpose of your email. The subject line should be concise and clear but still, grab the reader's attention.

After you have created a strong subject line, it is time to concentrate on the body. Your body should be concise, engaging, and well-written. It should also include all relevant information about your pitch. The body should contain a brief introduction to your company, a description of your product or service, and a request for investment.

Consider adding additional support materials, such as a pitch deck and executive summary, to your email pitch. This will make it even more persuasive. These supporting materials should be visually appealing and contain more information about your company and vision.

Remember that you must research potential investors before crafting an email pitch. You should tailor your message to meet their needs and interests. This will allow you to create a more personal and compelling pitch that is more likely to get their attention.

A compelling pitch email is an essential part of any investor outreach strategy. You can make an email stand out from the crowd and grab potential investors' attention with the right approach.

Build Professional Network to Reach Investors:

When it comes to reaching potential investors, building a professional network is crucial. Of course, a well-crafted pitch can win investors over, but a strong network that can introduce and refer can greatly increase your chances of getting an investment.

Attending industry events and conferences can be another great way to build professional network. These events provide a unique opportunity for entrepreneurs and investors to meet one another. These events are a great way to network with other entrepreneurs, investors, and industry experts.

You can also leverage your existing connections to grow your network. Reach out to your existing network to ask for referrals or introductions to potential investors. You should be clear about the type of investor you seek and give a brief overview of the business and investment goals.

LinkedIn and other online networking platforms can also help you expand your network. Join relevant groups and connect with industry professionals to build relationships and expand your reach.

Consider joining an incubator or accelerator program. These programs provide valuable support and resources like mentorship, investor access, and networking opportunities. In addition, a reputable program can help you build your credibility and increase your chances of getting an investment.

Building a professional network is key to reaching potential investors. To increase your investment chances, attend industry conferences and leverage existing relationships.

Collaborate with Industry Experts and Strategic Partners:

Collaboration with industry experts and strategic partners can help you expand your network and make it easier to reach potential investors. In addition, you can benefit from valuable resources such as industry connections, expertise, and industry knowledge that will help you improve your pitch and find potential investors.

Attending industry events, trade shows, and conferences is a great way to form strategic partnerships. These events offer a chance to meet other professionals in your field and explore possible partnerships with organizations and companies that share your values and goals.

Reaching out to thought leaders and industry experts in your field is another way to create strategic partnerships. You should look for people with a good reputation and track record of success in the industry. If you are interested in possible collaborations, reach out to them.

Once you have identified potential partners to work with, approach them professionally and respectfully. Communicate your goals and objectives and be open to feedback. As a result, you can create a strong network with industry professionals and strategic partners to help you achieve your goals and connect you with potential investors.

Hosting Investor Events & Webinars:

Hosting investor events, webinars, and social media and email pitches can be a great way to attract investors and promote your pitch. In addition, investors can meet you in person and have the chance to ask questions.

When planning an investor event, it is important to think about your target audience. What kind of information would they find most valuable? For example, it may be beneficial to highlight achievements or milestones or focus on specific aspects of your company or industry. You should also choose the right platform to host your event, regardless of whether it is a webinar or in-person.

Your webinar or investor event will have a greater impact if you promote it extensively through your professional network, social networks, and email marketing. Consider partnering with other industry organizations and businesses to reach an even larger audience. Be prepared to follow up with attendees following the event to answer any questions or further develop your relationships with potential investors.

Tracking Your Progress and Adjusting Your Strategy:

After implementing your outreach strategy, monitoring your progress and adjusting as necessary is important. This will help you ensure that your time and resources are effectively used to reach potential investors.

You can track your progress by keeping a log of all your outreach efforts. This includes the number of emails you sent, social media posts that were made, and events hosted. This will help you identify the most effective methods and adapt your strategy accordingly. You should also pay attention to feedback from potential investors. For example, you may need to modify your pitch or messaging if you see a theme in the concerns or questions they raise.

Feel free to try new strategies or tactics to reach investors. Investment landscapes are constantly changing. What worked earlier may not work now. You can increase your chances of attracting potential investors and eventually achieving your funding goals by being flexible and open to new ideas.

Marketing and promoting your pitch are crucial to attracting investor attention and securing funding. You can expand your reach by creating a solid outreach strategy that uses multiple channels such as email, social media, webinars, and networking events. Collaboration with industry experts and strategic partners can help you expand your reach and network.

You should track your progress regularly and adjust your strategy as necessary. Analysing your outreach efforts' effectiveness can help you identify which channels and strategies produce the best results. This will allow you to concentrate your resources and efforts on these areas. These tips will help you increase your chances of getting the funding you need.

Chapter 19
Making a Memorable Pitch

Storytelling and Other Techniques

Every day there are many pitches in the business world, all competing for investors' attention. It can be difficult to make an impact and stand out in a sea of noise. There are strategies and techniques that you can use to create a pitch that grabs attention and sticks with your audience long after the presentation ends. Storytelling is one such technique.

Storytelling has been an integral part of human communication for thousands of years. It is how we communicate information, ideas, and experiences. We all feel a connection to it on an emotional level. If done well, storytelling can help you create a memorable and powerful pitch. This chapter will explore storytelling as a technique that enables you to make an impressive pitch and leave a lasting impression.

Storytelling is Powerful in Your Pitch:

The power of storytelling is essential when delivering a pitch to investors. Complex ideas and information can be communicated in a memorable, relatable, and engaging way using storytelling.

Stories are what we respond to as humans. Stories have been part of our culture for thousands of years. Stories can inspire, motivate, or move us emotionally in ways that figures and facts cannot. If you can tell compelling stories, you can capture your audience's attention, keep them interested, and leave a lasting impression.

Storytelling can be used in investor pitches to make investors feel more connected with your company. Investors will be able to understand your company's values and mission by telling a story about why it does what it does. This can increase interest and engagement, which can lead to successful investments. You can also make your pitch memorable by using storytelling techniques. This can help you stand out and increase your chances of success.

Identify Your Unique Brand Story and Value Proposition:

Identifying your brand story and value proposition is crucial to create a memorable pitch. Your brand story is your narrative about who you are, what, and why you do it. Your story sets you apart and builds an emotional connection with your audience.

It would help if you asked important questions to identify your brand story and value proposition. What are your values and mission? How are you solving the problem? What is it that makes you different from other competitors? What is your ultimate benefit, and how can it help your customers?

These questions will enable you to identify your brand's unique story and value proposition. This will help you identify what is most important for your audience and what will resonate best with them. Once you have identified your brand story and value proposition, you can start to craft a pitch to communicate your message effectively.

Tailoring Your Pitch to Your Target Audience:

Understanding your audience is an absolute necessity for a successful pitch. It would help if you tailored your presentation to meet their needs. Do your research to find out more about the investors you are pitching, including their investment history, interests, communication styles, and other information.

Suppose you pitch to venture capitalists specializing in technology StartUps, for example. In that case, you will want to emphasize the unique features and benefits and show how your technology fills a market need. On the other hand, if you are pitching to angel investors, highlight the experience and expertise of your team.

It would help if you also considered investors' personalities and communication styles. For example, some investors prefer a more detailed presentation with financial projections and data. Others may be more comfortable with a creative pitch.

You can create an engaging presentation that appeals to potential investors by getting to know your audience and adapting your pitch accordingly.

Making Complex Concepts Accessible:

It is important to remember that investors may have a different level of understanding than you about your product's industry and technical aspects. It can be challenging to communicate complex concepts engagingly and clearly. To make difficult ideas more understandable, Metaphors and analogies can be helpful in a great way.

Metaphors are figures that use language to describe something in terms of another. Analogies compare two things to help explain a concept. Investors can be helped to understand your product or service through metaphors and analogies. For example, if you're pitching a new product in software, you might say, "Our product is like the Swiss Army Knife" - it can do many things. This allows the investor to see the versatility of your product and makes it easy for them to comprehend.

Analogies are more powerful than metaphors because they directly compare two things. For example, your product is similar to a car. It's meant to be a vehicle and can get you there. But it's also easy to drive. This analogy helps investors understand the fundamental function of your product and highlights the value proposition.

It is important to use metaphors and analogies that are both relevant and understandable. However, avoid using too many analogies and metaphors. This can make your pitch appear sloppy or unprofessional. But metaphors and analogies can still be powerful tools for investors to understand complex concepts if used effectively and sparingly.

Deliver Your Pitch with Confidence and Charisma:

It's not what you say that matters when it comes to pitching success. But how you say it can make all of the difference. Your message and how you present it can significantly impact your audience's perception of your business. To grab your audience's attention, conveying your message confidently and charismatically is important. This will keep them interested throughout the pitch.

When delivering your pitch, confidence is essential. You must believe in your business and communicate that belief to your audience. In addition, confidence makes you trustworthy and credible, which is important when convincing investors to invest.

Charisma is essential for delivering a successful pitch. Charismatic people can make people feel comfortable and connect with them. Your pitch will be more memorable and engaging if you exude charisma. This can increase your chances of getting an investment.

This chapter will discuss tips and techniques to deliver your pitch with confidence, charisma, and charm. In addition, we will discuss body language, tone of voice, and other factors that influence how your audience perceives. These skills will help you create memorable pitches that resonate with your audience.

Connecting with Investors by Using Emotional Appeal:

It's more than just presenting facts and figures when pitching investors. Investors are influenced by emotions when making decisions. Investors are looking for solid financials and a business plan and want to feel invested in the company they are investing in. Emotional appeal can help you connect with investors and convince them to invest in your vision.

Sharing your personal story and the journey that brought you to your business idea is one way to appeal to emotional appeal. Investors are interested in your motivation, the problem you are solving, and why it is important to you. You can build a relationship with investors by sharing your personal experiences. Investors are more likely to remember your pitch.

You can also highlight your company's positive impact on society and the environment to add emotional appeal. Companies that have positive social and environmental impacts are more attractive to investors. If your company has the potential to make a positive impact, make sure you emphasize it in your pitch.

Strong, positive language and tone can evoke emotions and generate excitement around your pitch. Investors are more likely to invest if they feel enthusiastic about your business idea.

However, emotions should be used in moderation. It can be seen as manipulative or insincere if you do it too often. Always strike the right balance between appealing emotionally and presenting a strong business case.

Emotional appeal can be an effective way to reach investors and get them involved in your business. You can create excitement and emotions by sharing your personal story and highlighting the benefits of your business.

Create a Strong Opening and Closing to Your Pitch:

Your pitch's opening and closing are critical moments that will make or break your impression on potential investors. Strong openings will grab investors' attention and set the tone for the rest. A strong closing will make a lasting impression on potential investors and seal the deal. This section will provide strategies and tips for writing powerful closing and opening statements to make your pitch stand out.

Your first impressions matter. The opening statement of your pitch can be your chance to make an everlasting impression on your audience. Start your pitch with a provocative question, bold statement, or bold statement that grabs attention. It could be an interesting fact, a shocking statistic, or an anecdote highlighting your company's problem. No matter your chosen approach, it should be relevant, compelling, and set the stage for your pitch.

Creating a powerful closing that leaves an impression on your audience is equally important. This is your last chance to present your case and convince investors to act. A memorable closing can be achieved by highlighting your key points and reiterating your value proposition in an engaging and clear way. A call to action may be a good idea to encourage investors to take the next steps, such as investing in your company or scheduling a follow-up meeting.

A story that supports your brand's story and value proposition is another way to make a strong closing. For example, you could tell a story about a customer who benefited from your product or how you overcame a challenge in your company. No matter what approach you choose, ensure it's relevant, authentic, and leaves an impression on your audience.

You must be concise, clear, and confident to create a strong closing and opening. You should practice your pitch until it feels natural and comfortable in front of an audience. Remember to highlight the unique value proposition that makes your business stand out. You can grab investors' attention by crafting a strong opening or closing and presenting compelling reasons why they should invest in your business.

Chapter 20
Developing a Winning Pitch Strategy

Aligning Your Goals and Objectives

A winning pitch strategy will help any business or entrepreneur attract investors. A well-crafted strategy can convey a unique value proposition and positively impact investors. It is crucial to align your objectives and goals with the investors to create a successful pitch strategy.

Defining your pitch goals and objectives before creating a strategy is important. For example, what are you trying to achieve? Do you want to get funding? Are you looking to establish relationships with investors? Are you trying to generate awareness about your business and interest? After identifying your goals, you can develop a pitching strategy aligned with them.

For a successful pitch, you need to thoroughly understand your company, your audience, and your competitors. You must know the strengths and weaknesses of your business, the challenges and opportunities facing your industry, and the preferences of your target investors. This information will help you create a pitch that emphasizes the unique value proposition for your business. It can also address any objections or concerns the investor may have and show why you're the best investment opportunity. This chapter will help you develop a pitch strategy that aligns with the goals and objectives of your investor.

Set Clear Goals and Objectives for Your Pitch:

You must first understand your goals and objectives to develop a winning strategy. Before crafting your pitch, decide what you want to achieve. For example, do you want to gain funding, new clients, or new partners? Determining your goals will allow you to tailor your pitch and tell a resonant story.

It's crucial to be realistic and specific when setting goals and objectives. Think about what you hope to achieve in the short and long term and how you will measure your success. You can use this to create a road map for your pitch and ensure you are on track to reach your goals.

Understanding Your Target Audience and Conducting Market Research:

Understanding your target audience and conducting market research is critical to developing a winning strategy. You must first understand your audience and their pain points, needs, and preferences before crafting your pitch. It would help if you did thorough research to gain insight into the market, competitors, and trends. To make your pitch more effective, you can tailor it to resonate with your investor's needs and tastes if you understand your target audience.

There are many ways to conduct market research. It can be done through online surveys, focus groups, interviews, and social media listening. Online surveys allow you to quickly and easily gather feedback from large groups of people. Focus groups and interviews can help you gain a deeper understanding of the preferences and needs of your audience. Social media listening is monitoring social media platforms to identify trends, sentiments, and feedback about your industry or product.

You can use the insights you've gained from your research to help you craft your pitch. For example, understanding your target audience will help you prepare a pitch that speaks directly to the pain points of that audience and highlights your unique value proposition.

How to Craft a Powerful Elevator Pitch:

A short, persuasive speech can be given in the time it takes to ride the elevator. Hence the name. An elevator pitch is a powerful and concise way to introduce your business or idea to potential customers or investors. Therefore, creating a well-crafted elevator speech that can open doors and provide opportunities is important.

You must create a powerful elevator pitch by distilling your idea or business into a concise, compelling message that captures your goal. The elevator pitch should be 30-60 seconds long and contain relevant and important information about your idea or business.

Your elevator pitch needs to be tailored to your target audience. It should highlight the most appealing aspects of your business or idea. You should be able to adapt it according to the audience you are speaking with and their priorities and interests.

Your audience should remember your elevator pitch and be impressed by it. Avoid jargon and technical language, which could confuse or turn off your audience. Instead, you can generate interest, create curiosity and attract potential customers or investors with a good elevator pitch.

Developing an Effective Message Framework:

After you have defined your goals and objectives, and done market research, now is the time to create a message frame for your pitch. A messaging framework is an organized way to articulate your key messages and value proposition concisely and clearly. As a result, you should be able to deliver your pitch confidently and consistently.

Start by defining the key message pillars. This is the main concept or idea that you wish to convey to your audience. Next, consider what makes your service or product unique and why that matters to your clients. Finally, your key message pillars will be based on your audience's challenges or pain points and how you can help them.

After identifying your key messages, it's time to create supporting messages. They are the details and proofs that support your main messaging pillars. These should prove why your product is the right solution for your audience.

Keep your message concise and clear. Avoid technical jargon and buzzwords your audience may not understand. Make sure you use simple language and that your message is easily understood. Your pitch should communicate your value proposition to your target audience in a manner that is easy to understand. Avoid using industry jargon and complex concepts.

Incorporate Data and Analytics into Your Pitch Strategy:

Integrating data and analytics in your pitch can give you a boost to your credibility. In addition, you can show that your business has a solid basis for growth by using data to back up your projections and claims.

Having reliable and accurate data before incorporating data and analytics in your pitch is crucial. For example, you may conduct market research or analyse industry trends to identify key metrics for your business.

You can create visual aids to support your pitch once you've identified the relevant data sources. For example, create graphs, charts, or other data visualizations to make complex information easier for your audience to understand.

Finding the right balance when incorporating data and analytics in your pitch is crucial. Don't overwhelm your audience with complex technical details, but you don't want to provide too little information. Instead, use key data points to support your message.

Align Your Pitch with Your Business Plan and Financial Projections:

When you are developing your pitch, make sure that it matches your business plan and your financial projections. Investors will want to know that you have an effective plan for using their money to grow your company and generate returns.

It is important to explain how your financial projections and business plan support your goals. Include how you intend to use funds raised from investment to reach your goals. For example, you are expanding your product range or increasing marketing efforts.

Your financial projections should also be realistic, supported by data and market research. Investors want to know that you understand your market and that your projections are based on reasonable assumptions.

By aligning your pitch to your financial projections and business plan, you can show investors you are well-prepared.

In addition, this will demonstrate your strategy for success and return on investment. As a result, you can build credibility and trust with investors and improve your chances of getting the funding needed to grow your company.

Addressing Investor Concerns and Objections:

Investors will have questions and concerns, no matter how convincing your pitch may be. It's important to identify and address investor concerns as early as possible. Investors may be concerned about the size of the marketplace, the level of competition, the experience of the team, or the ability to scale the business.

It would help if you had a strong response ready to address these concerns. You must articulate the market opportunities clearly and show how your business can capture a significant market share. You should also demonstrate that you understand your competitors and how they differ from yours.

The experience of the team is another common concern. Investors will want to know if the team has the expertise and skills to execute the business plan successfully. Prepare to discuss the experience and qualifications of each team member and how they complement one another.

Investors also consider scalability. Investors want to know if your business model can be scaled and grow quickly to meet customer demand. Prepare to explain the scalability of your business model and how you will handle growth.

Anticipating potential objections and concerns will allow you to prepare thoughtful responses which address the issues at hand. In addition, it shows you are well-versed in your business and prepared to face challenges.

Prepare for Different Types of Investor Presentations:

StartUps and entrepreneurs must be ready to deliver their pitches in different formats in today's global and fast-paced business environment. This includes virtual presentations and in-person ones. The content of your presentation should be consistent, but the format and delivery may need to change to fit the circumstances.

It's important to consider the limitations of virtual presentations and adapt your pitch accordingly. For example, consider including more visuals and less text and incorporating interactive elements to engage the audience. You should also test your technology to ensure your internet connection is reliable and stable. This will help you avoid any technical problems during your presentation.

A presentation in person, however, allows for a face-to-face exchange of views and will enable you to build a personal relationship with your audience. It's crucial to build rapport with your audience in this situation and use body language and tone of voice to communicate confidence and credibility. Consider the logistics, including the room's acoustics and seating arrangements, when deciding on your presentation style.

Preparing for different formats of investor presentations will help you ensure your pitch is engaging and effective, no matter the format. In addition, being well-prepared will allow you to make an impact, whether presenting in person or virtually.

How to Create a Comprehensive Pitch Deck:

A well-crafted deck is one of the most crucial elements of a winning strategy. A pitch deck is an illustrated presentation highlighting your pitch's main points. This includes your value proposition and market opportunity. It also contains financial projections and information about your team. The pitch deck comes in many forms. Most will have a combination of slides, graphs, and charts that help you convey your message clearly and effectively.

It is crucial to consider your audience when creating a pitch deck. Your pitch deck needs to be tailored to the specific interests and needs of the investors that you are targeting. Consider what information and questions they may be interested in. You can then structure your pitch to communicate your key messages best while addressing investor concerns.

A comprehensive pitch deck should have several sections. These include an introduction to your company, a summary of your value proposition, and an overview of the target market. It also includes a description of products or services and a breakdown of your financial projections. Each section should have a clear focus and include compelling images to illustrate your main points.

It is important to consider the layout and design of your presentation in addition to its content. Your pitch deck must be visually appealing with a consistent font and colour scheme. Use images and visuals to illustrate your points instead of using a lot of text. It would help if you practiced your presentation many times to deliver it confidently and smoothly.

A well-crafted deck of pitches can be an effective tool to attract investors and gain support for your company. You can improve your fundraising success by following these guidelines to create a compelling and comprehensive pitch deck.

Chapter 21
Collaborating with Cofounders and Advisors

A strong pitch team will help entrepreneurs secure funding and launch their businesses. It takes a group effort to create and deliver a successful pitch. The founder or CEO is the face of the business, but it's a team effort. Working with cofounders or advisors has several benefits. They can bring complementary skills and expertise and provide valuable feedback and insight.

It is not easy to build a pitch team. Considering each member's strengths, weaknesses, and roles is important. This chapter will discuss the importance of assembling a solid pitch team and offer practical tips on how to work effectively with cofounders and advisors. This chapter can help you build a pitch team, whether you're just starting or already pitching your company.

Identify the Key Roles in Your Pitch Team:

To build a powerful pitch team, it is important first to

identify the needed roles. Of course, the exact composition of your team will vary depending on the details of your pitch and business, but some key roles can be crucial for success.

You'll want a CEO or founder to communicate your company's vision and mission. In addition, this person must be comfortable in public speaking and should have a good understanding of your industry and market.

Also, hire a CFO or financial expert to assist with financial projections and fundraising. A CTO or technical leader may also be needed if your company relies heavily upon technology.

Depending on your pitch and industry, you should hire advisors or consultants. They can offer expertise and guidance. For example, you could hire individuals who have experience in sales, marketing, or other areas.

When building your team, consider your pitch and your company's needs. You can build a team by identifying key roles for your business's success.

Responsibilities and Expectations of Each Team Member:

Determining the responsibilities and expectations of each team member are critical to building a successful pitch team. After identifying the key roles for your pitching team, it's important to define each member's responsibilities and expectations clearly. This will ensure that everyone understands their role and that there are no confusions or overlaps in roles.

It is important to consider the expertise and strengths of each member when defining roles. For example, if you have a team member with specialized knowledge in financial modelling, give them the task of creating financial projections. If a team member is especially good at public speaking, you should give them the task of delivering the presentation.

Also, it is important to define the expectations of each member clearly. It is important to set deadlines for deliverables and establish communication protocols. Set clear expectations to ensure everyone is on the right track and there are no surprises.

Establishing a culture that encourages accountability in your pitch team is also important. Holding team members accountable for their actions and ensuring they fulfil their responsibilities is important. Regular check-ins keep everyone on the same page and help ensure everything goes according to plan.

Creating a Team of Diverse Backgrounds and Skills:

A successful pitch requires a team of people with complementary skills and backgrounds. A team of pitch professionals with complementary backgrounds and skills can add a new perspective to the pitch and make it more appealing to investors. Therefore, it's crucial to consider each member of the team's strengths and weaknesses and how they complement each other when building a team.

When building a team for a pitch, it is important to have varying backgrounds. Diverse backgrounds and experiences bring different perspectives and approaches to a pitch. A diverse team will also allow you to reach more potential investors interested in companies that commit to diversity and inclusion.

Start by identifying what skills and experience you will need to build a diverse and complementary team. Find team members with complementary skills and experience who share your passion for business. Reach out to your existing network to identify potential team members and advisors with the necessary skills and expertise. Use LinkedIn and other networking tools to broaden your search.

When building a team, everyone must understand their role and responsibilities. Clarify each member's responsibilities and expectations to avoid confusion or misunderstandings later. Communication and regular check-ins ensure that all team members work effectively towards a common goal.

Working with Cofounders to Create a Unified Pitch Message:

It is important to have a coherent and unified message when pitching to investors. Cofounders must work together in collaboration to create a pitch that is compelling and reflects their goals and vision. Cofounders working together can ensure the pitch is well-rounded and consistent while addressing key investor concerns and objections.

Cofounders must first agree on their company's vision and goals before developing a pitch message. Next, the cofounders should determine the key messages they wish to convey. These include their unique value proposition and target market. Ensure that all cofounders are on the same page and understand their roles in the pitch.

The cofounders can also work together to develop the structure and content for the pitch. Each member should contribute their unique expertise and skills. It is possible to brainstorm ideas, provide feedback, and refine the pitch together until it's clear, concise, and compelling.

Cofounders must be able to communicate and collaborate effectively to create a cohesive pitch message. Working together, and leveraging one another's strengths, can help cofounders create a pitch that effectively communicates their vision and addresses investor concerns. This will ultimately help them secure the funding needed to realize their ideas.

Identify Advisors with Industry Expertise and Experience:

Building a strong team by identifying and hiring advisors with relevant industry experience and expertise is important. Advisors bring knowledge and connections to your StartUp that will help it succeed, particularly in areas you or other team members need more experience. Look for advisors with a proven track record in your industry who can offer strategic advice on fundraising, product development, and sales and marketing.

It's crucial to define advisors' roles and responsibilities when recruiting them. It's important to communicate how frequently you expect to meet with advisors and the kind of feedback that you are looking for. Some advisors prefer to remain hands-off, while others want to be involved in the day-to-day operation. Before moving forward, make sure that everyone is on the same page.

When building your advisory group, it's important also to consider diversity. Search for advisors with different backgrounds, perspectives, and skills than the existing team. It can bring new ideas and perspectives into your StartUp. This can be very valuable in helping it grow and succeed. Open yourself up to suggestions and feedback from your advisors, and be ready to change your strategy as necessary.

Communicate Effectively While Pitching:

Communication is key to achieving your goals. You must set clear expectations for your team and provide regular updates. It would help if you also encouraged open communication. Regular meetings, progress reporting, and collaboration tools can help achieve this.

Communication is also about active listening, giving constructive feedback, and being open to new perspectives and ideas. This can foster a collaborative atmosphere where team members are motivated and feel valued to do their best work.

It's also important to create a culture of accountability, where each team member is responsible for their tasks and knows how their work impacts the pitch strategy. Regular check-ins and goal-setting keep everyone on the same page and ensure they work towards a shared vision.

You can make sure that your team is on the same page and understands their roles by communicating well. It can increase your chances of success and your presentation's effectiveness.

Create a Culture of Feedback and Improvement in Your Pitch Team:

Creating a culture that encourages feedback and continuous improvements within your team is important to build a winning presentation. A stronger, more effective pitch can be achieved by creating an environment where team members are comfortable sharing ideas, receiving and giving feedback, and working towards continuous improvement. In addition, creating a culture that encourages open communication, respect, and accountability in your team is important.

To promote a culture that encourages feedback, schedule regular team meetings to discuss progress, brainstorm new ideas, and address any challenges or concerns that may arise. Encourage team members to be honest and open when sharing their ideas and thoughts during these meetings. It's important for a leader to actively listen and give constructive feedback without being judgmental.

Setting clear goals and objectives can foster a culture that encourages continuous improvement. You can create a shared understanding by defining metrics and measurable goals for success. It can also keep team members motivated and focused to achieve the desired results.

It is also important to regularly evaluate the performance of your team. This will help you identify any areas that need improvement and can provide growth opportunities. Consider performing regular performance reviews and gathering feedback from team members and stakeholders to help your team grow professionally.

Creating a culture of continuous improvement and feedback within your pitch team will help you create a more successful and effective pitch. In addition, you can create a motivated team by encouraging open communication, accountability, and mutual respect.

Manage Conflicts and Challenges Within Your Pitching Team:

Conflicts and challenges will always arise in any collaborative effort. The pitch team is not an exception. Therefore, addressing and managing issues proactively is important to ensure the team stays productive and focused on creating a winning presentation. In addition, effective communication and conflict resolution skills are essential to managing challenges and conflicts that may arise in your pitch team.

A difference of opinion or disagreement about the strategy or approach to the pitch can be a common challenge within the team. It can be due to a need for alignment regarding goals and objectives or differences between individual perspectives and experiences. Create a culture where team members feel comfortable sharing their opinions and concerns. It is your job as a team leader to facilitate these discussions and guide the team toward a solution that aligns with the overall pitch strategy.

Certain team members' lack of motivation or commitment can also be challenging. As a team leader, it is important that you identify and deal with the root causes of this lack of commitment. It may mean reassigning responsibility or offering additional training or support to struggling team members.

Conflicts can also arise due to differences between team members regarding personalities or working styles. It can cause tension and even escalate to more serious issues that could disrupt the progress and productivity of the team.

Managing conflicts and challenges within your pitch team will require strong leadership skills, effective communication, and a commitment to cultivating a culture that encourages collaboration and continuous improvement. You can keep your team motivated and focused by constructively addressing issues.

Building a solid pitch team is crucial for delivering a compelling pitch. For a team to succeed, it's important to define all team members' roles, responsibilities, and expectations. Building a team of complementary people with different skills and backgrounds is also crucial. Finally, to maintain a productive and positive working environment, managing the team's conflicts and challenges is important. By investing in a team of pitch professionals, StartUps and entrepreneurs can improve their chances of securing funding.

Chapter 22
Overcoming Pitching Challenges

Common Obstacles and How to Overcome Them

Pitching is a crucial part of growing your StartUp or as an entrepreneur. It will help you to secure funding, build partnerships, and grow your business. Pitching can be stressful and challenging, even though it is important. A pitch can be fraught with obstacles, from technical issues to unexpected investor questions.

To overcome these challenges, you need to combine preparation, adaptability, and resilience. Understanding the obstacles that are most likely to arise during pitching and how to overcome them will increase your chances for success and help you effectively communicate your business' value.

This chapter will provide tips and strategies to overcome the most common challenges in pitching. This chapter is for all entrepreneurs, whether you're a seasoned founder or a newbie. It will give you the tools to deliver a successful pitch and reach your business goals.

Handling Anxiety and Nervousness:

Anxiety and nervousness are two of the biggest obstacles entrepreneurs and founders face when pitching their ideas. Although it's normal to be a little nervous before a presentation, if this feeling becomes overwhelming, the performance of the presenter and the pitch can suffer.

You can deal with anxiety and nervousness while pitching in many ways, and first, practicing your pitch several times before the presentation is crucial. Then, the presenter will become more familiar and comfortable with the material.

Before the game, you can also benefit from mindfulness meditation or relaxation exercises. These techniques can reduce anxiety and help promote calmness and focus. Other anxiety control techniques include deep breathing, positive affirmations, and visualization.

Remember that your audience is on your side. Investors want to see your success. They are searching for promising StartUps. An audience member's friendly smile or nod can ease nerves and boost confidence.

How to Handle Difficult Questions and Objections from Investors:

The pitching process will always include handling difficult questions or objections. Investors may ask challenging questions that make you uncomfortable, feel caught off guard, or unsure how to answer. To handle these situations successfully, you must be confident and prepared.

Research the investor you pitch to and their investment preferences and track record. You can prepare for their questions and objections by doing thorough research on them, their investment preferences, and their track record.

Listen carefully to what the investor says and spend time understanding their needs. You can then tailor your answer to meet their needs and concerns. In addition to active listening and preparation, stay calm and composed when answering difficult questions or objections. Keep eye contact and respond confidently and clearly. Take a deep breath. Investors want to know how you respond under pressure or in difficult situations. So, remaining calm and confident will work for you.

It is crucial to be transparent and honest if you cannot answer a specific question or respond to an objection. You can acknowledge that you don't have an answer now but promise to follow up with the investor when you have more details. This shows your commitment to transparency and willingness to work with the investor to address their concerns.

How to Adapt to Unexpected Changes in the Pitch:

Every successful pitcher should be able to adapt to unexpected changes. You may have practiced your delivery and prepared your pitch deck, but unexpected changes, such as changes in speaker order or technical problems, can still occur. Therefore, it is important to remain flexible and keep a positive outlook when facing these changes.

Practice your pitch in various environments and scenarios. For example, you can practice your pitch in front of colleagues or friends who can give feedback or simulate distractions. In addition, you can practice in different settings, such as a conference room, a boardroom, or even a small one to get used to the pitching environment.

Prepare backup plans as another way to adapt to unexpected changes. For example, if your pitch heavily relies on visual aids, but the projector fails, you must be prepared to present it without slides. Likewise, you should be ready to adapt your presentation if the order of the pitches changes.

It is also important to stay calm and composed when unexpected changes occur. Take a deep breath and collect your thoughts. Then continue with your pitch. It would help if you remembered that changes are inevitable and can occur to anyone. How you respond to them will show your professionalism and ability to adapt to unexpected situations.

Overcome Language and Cultural Barriers:

The language barrier and cultural differences can be major obstacles when pitching to international investors. Understanding your audience's values, culture, and communication preferences is important to overcome these barriers. This will allow you to tailor your message to resonate with your audience and help avoid cultural faux pas.

Avoiding industry jargon or technical terms is a great way to overcome the language barrier. Consider hiring a professional interpreter or translator to convey your message correctly.

Understanding the local regulatory and business landscape is also important when pitching international investors. This can help you tailor your pitch to address the concerns and challenges of investors in that particular region.

It's important to build trust with international investors and establish strong relationships. You can achieve this by showing a genuine interest and respect for their culture and values. Also, it would help if you were willing to adapt and learn. Finally, the time and effort invested in developing these relationships will pay off.

How to Address Any Weaknesses or Gaps in Your Pitching Strategy:

Even if you spend a lot of time and energy preparing your pitch, it may still have some gaps or weaknesses. Early identification of these gaps and the subsequent steps taken to close them can make all the difference in a successful pitch or a missed opportunity. These are some common weaknesses or gaps in pitching strategies:

Uncertainty: Investors can feel uneasy about your business if you give an unclear or confusing pitch. Your message must be clear and concise to address this issue. To get feedback, practice your pitch in front of colleagues or friends unfamiliar with your business.

Investors are looking for data to support your business model and projections demonstrating the growth potential. In addition, you may seek additional expertise or research if your data or projections need to be more convincing or complete.

Investors are looking for investors who have done adequate market research. They want to see that you know your market well and have a plan to capture market share. You may research the market or your competitors to improve your pitch.

Investors are looking for a team with high competence and commitment to success. If you have a weak team or one lacking the relevant experience to make a good pitch, hiring additional team members or finding advisors who will help strengthen your pitch might be necessary.

Investors are looking for differentiation. If you do not differentiate your company from the competition, it is important to review your messaging and value proposition to make sure that your unique selling point is communicated.

It is essential to be willing to accept feedback to improve your pitch.

How to Deal With Tough Competition from Other StartUps:

Entrepreneurs often face the challenge of navigating tough competition when they pitch to investors. Developing a strategy that will help you stand out amongst the many StartUps competing for limited funding is crucial. It's important to have a solid strategy to help you stand out from the competition.

Focusing on your unique value proposition is a great way to attract investors. It will help you make your business the best investment option. You can do this by showcasing your team's expertise and experience, innovative new technology, or showing early success and traction in the market.

A second strategy is to find collaborators or potential partners that can help you use their strengths and resources to improve your product. For example, it may be necessary to form strategic alliances with StartUps in your field, partner with established companies, or engage with thought leaders or key influencers who can help gain credibility and visibility in the market.

To succeed in a constantly changing market, you need to be persistent, resilient, and adaptable. You can position your StartUp for success by staying focused on your goals and refining your pitch.

How to Find Balance between Confidence and Humility:

Many entrepreneurs struggle to balance confidence and humility when pitching their StartUp idea to investors. Confidence is important to show your passion for your business and your conviction. On the other hand, overconfidence can be perceived as arrogance and may turn away potential investors. Find a good balance between the two. Be humble and acknowledge the risks and challenges of your business.

To achieve balance, you can highlight the strengths and achievements of your StartUp and acknowledge areas that need improvement. Investors will want to know that you understand the risks involved and have a plan in place to minimize them. Openness to feedback is important, as well as a willingness to listen to the concerns and suggestions of investors.

You can also show humility by recognizing the expertise and experience of your team while acknowledging those who have assisted you, like advisors, partners, or mentors. This shows you're not just focused on your success but also appreciate the support from others.

Finding the balance between humility and confidence takes self-awareness and practice. You can improve your ability to convey your message by seeking feedback, reflecting upon your performance, and continually improving your pitch.

How to Deal With Rejections and Learn From Failed Pitches:

Entrepreneurs must learn to deal with rejection from them. Even the most successful entrepreneurs will face rejection, which can be difficult to swallow. However, please remember that rejections are part of the pitching and learning process.

Rejection can be used as a chance to get feedback from investors. Understanding why investors rejected your pitch will help you identify improvement areas and refine the pitch strategy for future opportunities. It is also important to remain positive and motivated, as the road to success is not always straight.

It would help if you also learned from your failed pitches to improve your pitching strategy. Take your time to identify what went wrong with your pitch and where you can improve. Ask your pitch team for feedback and your advisors to give you valuable insight on how to improve.

Remember that rejection does not mean the end. Continue to refine your pitch strategy and find new opportunities to present your business. You can learn from a failed business pitch by being resilient, persistent, and willing to accept mistakes.

How to Build Resilience and Perseverance in the Face of Pitch Challenges:

It can be difficult and stressful to pitch to investors. Even if you have a well-prepared pitch, it is possible to be rejected, face difficult questions or experience unexpected changes. Entrepreneurs who want to succeed need to be resilient and persistent. This will help them overcome setbacks and remain focused on their goals.

The mind-set is one of the most crucial factors in building resilience. Entrepreneurs with a growth mind-set are more likely than others to see challenges as an opportunity to improve and learn. They view rejection and failure as a part of the process and use it as feedback to improve their pitch strategy.

A support network is another key element in building resilience. Co-founders and advisors, mentors, or peers from the StartUp community can be included. In addition, a sounding board can help entrepreneurs remain motivated and focused throughout the pitching process. They can bounce ideas off, get feedback and share their experiences.

Persistence is crucial when it comes to overcoming challenges in a pitch. Persistent entrepreneurs are more likely than others to continue despite obstacles and setbacks. They know that success is often achieved through multiple attempts and are willing to push until they reach their goals.

Entrepreneurs can build persistence by setting goals for themselves and the pitch team. They should also establish a timeline and track their progress. Celebrate small wins along the way to a larger goal. This can keep motivation and momentum going.

Resilience and perseverance are essential to success in the presentation process. Entrepreneurs with a growth mind-set, who leverage their support networks, and keep a constant focus on their goals, are more likely to achieve success both in their business and their pitches.

It is not easy to pitch your StartUp successfully. You can encounter many obstacles along the way, including nervousness, anxiety, objections, difficult questions, and tough competition and rejection. However, you can overcome these challenges with the right strategy and mind-set. You can build the resilience and perseverance you need to be successful in the high-pressure environment of StartUp pitches by taking the time to thoroughly prepare, regularly practicing your pitch, asking for feedback from your pitch team, advisors, and pitch team, and learning from mistakes. Each challenge is an opportunity for you to grow and improve your strategy. You can overcome any obstacle with determination and perseverance and reach your pitching goals.

Chapter 23
Building Long-Term Partnerships

Strategies to Build and Nurture Investor Relationships

Building investor relationships is essential to any Startup's success. These relationships can be a valuable source of guidance, expertise, and networking opportunities. They are also a great way to raise money. However, it would help if you had more than a great pitch to develop and maintain strong relationships with investors. To nurture long-term relationships, you need a strategic approach.

Relationships with investors take time to build. It takes time and effort for you to build trust and credibility. Entrepreneurs must go beyond simply pitching their ideas and instead focus on building trust and mutual respect. This chapter will examine the importance of developing investor relationships and offer strategies to entrepreneurs for nurturing these partnerships to achieve long-term success.

Importance of Long-Term Relationships:

A StartUp must understand the importance of long-term relationships. Investors can be a valuable source of advice, guidance, and connections for a company. In addition, a strong relationship with investors will help StartUps to secure additional funding for expansion and growth.

A long-term relationship can also provide stability to a StartUp. A group of investors committed to the business's goals and vision can give a StartUp a sense of security.

Investors also can provide credibility and validation for a StartUp. Investors who publicly associate with a company can build its brand and reputation. A StartUp with a large network of investors will also attract more investors and partners. This increases its visibility and success potential.

In general, any StartUp that wants to be successful in the long term must understand the importance of long-term relationships. Focusing on developing strong relationships with investors will help StartUps secure the capital, guidance, and support they need to grow and flourish.

Maintaining Regular Communication with Investors:

Maintaining regular communication is essential to building long-lasting investor relationships. Maintaining open lines of communication with investors is important once you have found the right ones for your StartUp. This will inform them about your challenges, plans, and progress.

Regular communication can be in many formats, including email updates, phone conversations, videoconferences, and meetings in person. Communication frequency and format can differ depending on your Startup's stage and investors' preferences. For example, investors may want regular updates, while others prefer only to receive information when major milestones are reached.

Responding to investor concerns and questions is also part of effective communication. Therefore, it is important to respond to your investors' questions and concerns promptly, transparently, and thoroughly to help you build trust and credibility with your investors and demonstrate your commitment to a long-term relationship with them.

Regular communication is key to building long-lasting investor relationships and ensuring your StartUp gets the support needed to grow and prosper.

Creating a Plan for Ongoing Engagement:

Creating a plan for ongoing engagement and relationship-building with investors is crucial for StartUps seeking long-term partnerships. A clearly defined plan can establish a framework for collaboration, communication, and shared goals. This plan may include regular company performance updates, information on new products and services, or upcoming milestones or events.

A successful engagement plan must be tailored to meet the needs and interests of every investor. Creating personalized messages, reports, and updates tailored to each investor's specific investment interests, industry focus, or geographical location is possible.

Establishing clear communication channels and expectations is another important part of a plan. Depending on investor preferences and availability, this could include regular video or phone calls, email updates, or in-person meetings. In addition, StartUps can use technology platforms, like investor portals and online reporting tools, to streamline communication.

An engagement plan can include opportunities for investors

to attend company events such as product launches or trade shows in addition to regular communications. This can help build stronger relationships and deepen investor understanding of company values, mission, and vision.

Creating a plan for ongoing engagement and relationship-building with investors helps establish a strong foundation for long-term partnerships, promotes investor confidence and trust, and fosters mutual success and growth.

Transparency and honesty are Key to Building Trust with Investors:

Building long-term relationships requires building trust and credibility. Investors are looking for a StartUp that is transparent and honest about its progress and challenges. To achieve this, StartUps need to be honest and transparent with investors throughout the relationship-building process.

Investors' trust can be created by providing regular updates and reports on progress. Monthly or quarterly reports can highlight key metrics, achievements, and setbacks or challenges. Transparency will help investors to understand the risks and rewards associated with investing in a StartUp.

Investors should also be told the truth about any problems or obstacles. StartUps should not try to hide problems. Instead, they should face them and work with investors on solutions. This shows the founders are committed to the Startup's success and will take full responsibility for any failures.

Transparency about the financials of the company and its fundraising goals is another way to establish trust and credibility. Investors are looking for a StartUp that has a plan to use their money and will return their investment. By being transparent about their company's financials and fundraising goals, they can demonstrate to investors that they're serious about building a business.

Developing trust and credibility with investors requires honesty and transparency throughout the relationship-building process. StartUps can establish trust with investors by being transparent and open about their company's financials, progress, and challenges.

How to Navigate Difficult Conversations with Investors and Manage Conflicts:

Building strong and lasting investor relationships requires navigating difficult conversations with investors and managing conflicts. Investors can have different goals, expectations, and opinions than founders. Conflicts can occur when there is an inability to communicate or understand.

To avoid conflict, having an open and honest dialog with investors is important. Transparency is key in addressing any questions or concerns that investors might have. In addition, maintaining a solution-focused attitude and working with investors to find mutually beneficial solutions when conflicts arise is crucial.

If necessary, hire a third-party mediator or advisor who can help resolve conflicts and reach a solution that is beneficial to both parties. The ultimate goal is to ensure that StartUp goals and vision are aligned with the investors and maintain a positive, productive relationship. By proactively addressing conflict and encouraging open and transparent communication with investors, founders can create strong, lasting relationships.

Evaluate and Adjust Your Investor Relations Strategy Over Time:

Building long-term relationships with investors requires continually evaluating and adjusting your investor relationship strategies. Investor needs and goals will change as your

StartUp grows. Therefore, regularly assess your investor relationships and ensure they align with your current needs.

It would help if you established clear metrics to evaluate the success of your investor relationships. Among others, these metrics may include financial performance and strategic partnerships. You can track your progress and gain insights into your investor relationships by tracking these metrics.

After establishing your metrics, you should review your investor relations regularly to see if they are contributing to the success of your StartUp. This could include analysing your level of communication and engagement with investors and their value to your StartUp. This analysis will help you identify areas needing improvement and adjust your investor relations strategy.

Diversifying your investor pool and seeking out investors with unique perspectives or expertise can be part of adjusting your strategy. Focus on investors offering long-term stability and support instead of those looking for short-term gains.

The key to successfully evaluating your investor relations strategy and making adjustments is to be agile and responsive to your Startup's changing needs. In addition, you can help your StartUp grow and succeed by building relationships with investors.

Promoting Open Communication and Transparency:

It is important to foster open communication and transparency to build strong relationships with investors. This involves creating a safe environment for investors to express their opinions and concerns and for the StartUp to be transparent with its investors.

Open communication with investors can build trust and credibility and foster a partnership between the StartUp company and its investors. In addition, open communication can help identify issues before they become serious problems and facilitate mutually beneficial solutions.

StartUps should set up regular communication channels with investors to foster transparency and open communication. For example, they could provide monthly or quarterly updates about the company's financial statements and plans. Responding to investor concerns and inquiries in a timely manner is important, as it shows a commitment to transparency.

A key element of open communication and transparency involves being honest and forthcoming with your Startup's challenges and setbacks. It can be tempting for investors to see a rosy picture, but this could ultimately damage the relationship if reality does not match expectations. Instead, StartUps should be transparent with their successes and challenges and collaborate with investors to create strategies that address these.

Fostering open communication and transparency are key to building long-term relationships. By creating a mutually respectful and trusting environment, StartUps will be able to receive the guidance and support they need to reach their goals.

Solicit Feedback from Investors and Incorporate Their Input into Your Strategy:

You can seek investors' perspectives and insights on important business decisions and strategies. You can build stronger relationships with your investors by asking for feedback. This will help you to understand their expectations and needs better. Listening to your investors' feedback is crucial. This will help you make better decisions and align your interests with theirs.

You must be open and transparent when soliciting feedback from investors. You should also provide them with concise and clear information about the business and its progress. It can build trust with your investors and increase the likelihood that they'll provide valuable feedback. Prepare to answer any questions or concerns your investors might have and provide regular updates about your achievements and progress.

Investor input can be incorporated into your strategy by making changes to your business plan, product roadmap, or financial projections. In addition, you can develop a strategy that better meets the expectations and needs of your investors by incorporating their feedback into your decision-making process. Finally, by actively seeking and incorporating investor feedback, you can demonstrate your commitment to building long-term partnerships based on trust and collaboration.

Setting realistic expectations with investors and managing expectations:

To build long-term relationships, managing expectations and setting realistic goals is important. Transparency is key when seeking investment. Be transparent about the current state of your StartUp, its plans, and any potential challenges. It would help if you also understood your investors' goals and expectations for their investment.

It would help to communicate your goals to investors to manage expectations. It will ensure that everyone works towards the same goals and is on the same page. It would help if you also were realistic regarding the time frame for reaching these goals and any obstacles or risks that might arise.

Set expectations for the level of communication and involvement that your investors will receive from your StartUp. Establish clear communication channels and be clear about meetings, and update frequency. This will build trust between the two parties and prevent misunderstandings.

It's also important to be upfront about your Startup's progress toward its goals. It's best to be honest, and upfront with investors if you face unexpected setbacks or challenges, rather than try to minimize or hide the issue. You can overcome obstacles with your investors by being honest and open.

Building strong relationships with investors will be crucial to the success of your StartUp. Both parties must be willing to put in the effort and time. Some strategies StartUps can use to foster long-term partnerships understand the importance of long-term relationships with investors, identifying the best investors, creating a plan of ongoing engagement, building trust and credibility, and navigating difficult discussions.

StartUps can establish trust with investors by fostering an open dialogue and transparency. This will help them build a solid foundation for a relationship that will last a long time. Incorporating investor feedback into the strategy and soliciting feedback can help StartUps align their objectives with investors' expectations and create a mutually beneficial relationship. It is important to manage expectations and set realistic goals for investors to avoid miscommunications and conflicts. Remember that building investor relationships is a continuous process and requires constant attention.

StartUps that build strong relationships with investors will benefit from the financial support and the strategic advice, networks, and expertise they can offer. These partnerships help StartUps overcome the challenges of scaling up their business and lead to long-term growth.

Chapter 24
Pitching to Venture Capitalists

Unique Considerations and Best Practices

Pitching to venture capital (VC) firms can be crucial for StartUps looking to secure funding and grow their business. However, the process can be complex and daunting, with unique considerations and best practices to follow. In addition, unlike other types of investors, venture capitalists generally seek high-growth, scalable companies with the potential for significant returns on investment. As a result, StartUps need to approach their pitch to venture capitalists with a strategic mind-set and a deep understanding of the industry and the expectations of this type of investor.

This chapter will explore unique considerations and best practices for presenting to venture capitalists. We will discuss the importance of thoroughly researching potential VC firms and understanding their criteria and investment approach. We'll also look at the key elements of an effective pitch, including the pitch deck, financial projections, and management team.

Additionally, we will dive deeper into the due diligence process and how StartUps can prepare for and navigate this critical phase of the investment process. Finally, we will discuss the post-investment relationship with venture capitalists and how StartUps can manage this relationship for long-term success.

Role of venture capitalists in financing StartUps:

VC firms can be a great source of funding for StartUps. Unlike traditional bank loans or other forms of financing, VC is a type of investment in which investors provide funds to StartUps in exchange for equity in the business. Venture capitalists typically invest in high-growth companies with innovative ideas or disruptive technologies that can generate significant returns on investment. In addition to funding, venture capitalists also provide strategic advice, mentorship, and access to their networks of industry contacts, which can help StartUps achieve their goals and scale their businesses faster. Understanding the role of venture capitalists in funding StartUps is critical for entrepreneurs considering this type of funding as a way to fuel their growth.

Unique Requirements and Expectations of VC Pitches:

Preparing for the unique requirements and expectations of VC presentations is crucial for any StartUp seeking funding from VC firms. Venture capitalists have distinct criteria to evaluate potential investments and proposals, and founders must know these expectations before approaching them. The focus on growth potential and scalability are among the main factors distinguishing VC presentations from other funding presentations. Venture capitalists look for StartUps that have the potential to grow quickly and become market leaders in their respective industries. As such, StartUps must have a clear and compelling growth strategy demonstrating their ability to achieve high growth rates.

Another key consideration is the amount of funding sought. Venture capitalists typically invest large sums of money in StartUps, and as such, they expect a high degree of due diligence and preparation from founders. As a result, StartUps seeking VC funding should have a well-developed business plan, financial projections, and a clear understanding of the market opportunity they are targeting. Additionally, StartUps must demonstrate that they have a strong team capable of executing the company's growth strategy.

In addition to these requirements, VC pitches often involve multiple funding rounds, each with its expectations and requirements. Founders should be aware of the different funding stages and the criteria used to evaluate StartUps at each stage. They should also have a clear understanding of the terms and conditions of the financing being offered, including the equity stake that is being waived and any restrictions or covenants related to the funding.

Preparing a VC pitch requires thoroughly understanding venture capitalists' unique requirements and expectations. Founders must demonstrate a scalable business model, a strong team, and a clear cut growth-path and profitability. StartUps must also be prepared to answer tough questions and provide detailed financial and operational data to support their case. By doing so, founders can increase their chances of securing funding from VC firms and put their StartUps on the path to success.

A Pitch Deck That Resonates with Venture Capitalists:

Crafting a pitch deck that resonates with venture capitalists is critical to pitching successfully to venture capitalists. Venture capitalists usually receive many arguments and have limited time to consider them. Therefore, a well-designed pitch deck that captures their attention and effectively conveys your Startup's value proposition is essential.

The pitch deck should include key elements such as a problem statement, market opportunity, solution overview, business model, competitive landscape, team biographies, financial projections, and demand. However, it is important to tailor the pitch deck to the specific VC firm you are targeting. Different companies may have unique requirements or preferences for pitch deck content and formatting.

Additionally, venture capitalists may look for different criteria than other investors, such as a strong emphasis on growth potential and scalability. Therefore, it is important to research the specific VC firm you are targeting and tailor your pitch to align with their investment strategy and portfolio.

Designing a compelling pitch deck involves striking the right balance between being concise and providing enough detail to demonstrate your Startup's potential. A successful pitch deck should tell a story and engage the audience, highlighting your Startup's unique value proposition and potential. However, it's also important to have a clear and concise call to action, outlining what you are asking for and what you hope to achieve from the investment.

Crafting a pitch deck that resonates with venture capitalists involves tailoring the content and format to the specific company, highlighting your Startup's unique value proposition and potential. , and strike the right balance between being concise and providing enough detail to demonstrate potential.

Build Relationships with Venture Capitalists:

When it comes to pitching to venture capitalists, relationship building is crucial. It is important to remember that venture capitalists invest in people as much as they invest in ideas. Therefore, they want to work with passionate, dedicated founders with a clear vision for growing their StartUps.

To build these relationships, founders must attend industry events, network with venture capitalists, and seek pitches from mutual relationships. They should also take the time to research and understand the investment criteria of each VC firm they present to, tailoring their presentation to align with the firm's focus areas and investment strategies.

Venture capitalists have specific presentation requirements and expectations that differ from those of other investors. They are looking for StartUps with high growth potential, a scalable business model, and a clear path to profitability. Founders should be prepared to discuss the size of their market opportunity, their competitive landscape, and the expertise and experience of their team.

Venture capitalists often expect a high level of due diligence and financial analysis from StartUps. As a result, founders should be prepared to share detailed financial projections, a clear plan for using investment funds, and a thorough understanding of their Startup's financial metrics.

Building relationships with venture capitalists takes time and effort but can pay off in the long run. Even if a particular VC firm isn't investing in a Startup's current cycle, it may still be interested in future cycles or offer valuable advice and mentorship. By understanding venture capitalists' investment criteria and tailoring presentations to their specific needs, founders can increase their chances of securing funding and building long-term relationships with valuable partners.

Demonstrate a Viable ROI Path for Venture Capitalists:

One key consideration when pitching to venture capitalists is demonstrating a viable path to return on investment (ROI) for investors. Venture capitalists look for StartUps that have the potential to generate significant returns on investment in a relatively short time frame, typically three to seven years. As such, StartUps must have a clear and well-defined plan to use investment funds to grow the business and generate profits.

To demonstrate a viable path to ROI, StartUps must articulate a clear business plan outlining their market opportunities, competitive landscape, and growth potential. This plan should include a detailed financial model that shows how the StartUp plans to generate revenue and profit over time. StartUps must also be able to provide evidence of market validation, such as customer attraction or partnerships with established industry players.

StartUps must be prepared for any potential risks or challenges that may impact their ability to generate a return on investment. For example, StartUps in highly regulated industries may need help obtaining approvals or complying with regulatory requirements. In addition, StartUps that rely on a single vendor or partner may face risks related to supply chain disruptions or other issues.

Demonstrating a viable path to ROI is essential to pitching to venture capitalists. StartUps that clearly articulate their business plan and growth potential while addressing potential risks and challenges are more likely to attract attention and investment from venture capitalists.

Develop a Clear and Realistic Valuation of Your StartUp:

Developing a clear and realistic valuation for your StartUp is an essential step in preparing to pitch to venture capitalists. The appraisal is the estimated value of your business, and it is essential to understand how the value of your business was calculated. In addition, it is essential to understand that valuation is both an art and a science and that several methods exist to calculate it. However, a too high or low valuation can hurt your pitch.

One approach to valuing a StartUp is to estimate the total addressable market (TAM) and calculate the potential revenue that could be generated. Other methods include comparing your company to similar StartUps or analysing your company's financial projections. StartUps must clearly understand their business's finances and projections, including revenue, expenses, and growth potential. In addition, it would be helpful to consider the competitive landscape and potential risks when determining your business valuation.

Venture capitalists generally look for a significant return on investment and expect a clear path to profitability and growth for your business. Therefore, a realistic valuation that aligns with your business finances and growth potential will demonstrate that you have a solid understanding of your business and the market.

Being transparent and open to feedback during the evaluation process is also important. Venture capitalists may have different perspectives and criteria for assessing the value of your business, and it's critical to listen to their feedback and consider how it aligns with your business goals and projections. Ultimately, a clear and realistic valuation can help build your credibility with venture capitalists and increase your chances of securing funding.

Managing Capital and Ownership Considerations in VC Transactions:

Managing capital and ownership considerations in VC transactions is critical to securing funding from venture capitalists. Typically, venture capitalists invest in StartUps in exchange for equity or equity in the business. This means that founders and early investors may need to dilute their stake in the StartUp to secure the necessary funding.

Therefore, StartUp founders need to have a clear idea of

how much capital they are willing to give up in exchange for funding, as well as the impact this will have on their ownership and control of the business.

It is also essential to negotiate favourable terms and conditions in the agreement, such as anti-dilution protections and liquidation preferences.

Additionally, StartUp founders should carefully consider the long-term implications of any capital or ownership deals, as they can affect the company's ability to attract future investors and retain key talent. It is important to strike a balance between obtaining the necessary financing and maintaining sufficient ownership and control to grow the business and achieve its goals.

Managing equity and ownership considerations in VC transactions requires ongoing planning, negotiation, and communication with investors. Therefore, StartUps should work closely with legal and financial advisors to make informed decisions and get the best possible terms for their business.

Negotiate Term Sheet and Conclusion of the Agreement:

Negotiating the term sheets and closing the deal with venture capitalists is essential in securing your Startup's investment. A term sheet is a non-binding agreement outlining the terms and conditions of the investment, including valuation, ownership, and investor and StartUp rights. It serves as the framework for the final agreement and is negotiated between the parties before the actual investment occurs.

Negotiating the term sheet requires a good understanding of key terms and how they will affect ownership and control of your StartUp. It is important to fully understand the investor's expectations and goals for the investment and your own. This can include board composition, control, and founder acquisition.

Once the term sheet is agreed, it's time to close the deal. This involves finalizing the deal and signing all the necessary legal documents, including the investment and shareholders' agreements. Again, working with an experienced legal advisor is important to ensure that the transaction is structured appropriately and that all legal requirements are met.

Closing the deal is also an opportunity to build a strong relationship with your venture capitalist. Therefore, it is important to communicate regularly with your investor and keep them informed of the progress of your StartUp. This can help build confidence in your ability to execute your business plan and generate a return on investment.

Negotiating term sheets and closing deals with venture capitalists requires careful preparation, clear communication, and a solid understanding of the key terms and considerations. By approaching the process strategically and working with experienced advisors, StartUps can secure the funding they need to grow and thrive.

Different Stages of VC Funding:

Understanding the different stages of VC funding and what investors seek at each stage is key to pitching to venture capitalists successfully. VC funding usually takes place in stages, each representing a different level of investment and risk. Stages include Seed Funding, Seed Funding, Growth Funding, and Later Stage Funding.

At the seed funding stage, investors seek innovative and unique ideas with high growth potential, solid business plans and early traction in the market. As a result, they are often willing to take a higher risk in exchange for the possibility of a better return on investment. At this stage, StartUps are usually in the ideation or product development phase and have yet to generate significant revenue.

StartUps at seed funding stage have typically launched their product or service and started generating revenue, although they may still need to be profitable. Investors at this stage are looking for StartUps with strong growth potential and a clear path to profitability.

In the growth-stage funding stage, investors seek out StartUps that have already achieved significant growth and have a proven business model. StartUps at this stage typically generate significant revenue and can be profitable. Investors at this stage are looking for StartUps with a clear plan to scale their operations and continue to grow their market share.

In the later stage of funding, investors look for well-established companies with a proven track record of success. StartUps at this stage are usually market leaders in their industry and have already achieved significant revenue and profitability. Investors at this stage are looking for StartUps that can continue to grow and maintain their market position.

Understanding what investors seek at each VC funding stage is essential for StartUps seeking funding. By tailoring their pitch and demonstrating their potential for growth and profitability at every stage, StartUps can easily secure funding and build successful long-term partnerships with venture capitalists.

Potential Trade-offs Between Financing, Control, and Ownership:

Negotiating the terms of the deal with venture capitalists is crucial in securing funding for your StartUp. Remember that each term of an agreement comes with trade-offs that can impact both funding and control. As a founder, you need to weigh each term's potential pros and cons to help you make the best decision for your Startup's future.

One of the key trade-offs in VC deals is the balance between funding, control, and ownership. Venture capitalists typically invest in StartUps in exchange for equity in the business, meaning they own part of the business. Therefore, the more funding you receive, the more equity you will have to give up. This can impact your control over the business and potentially limit your ability to make decisions.

When negotiating the terms of the deal, it's important to consider the amount of capital you're willing to give up and the level of control you're comfortable with. For example, if you are confident in your ability to grow the business and don't want to give up too much control, you should trade a smaller investment with less equity. On the other hand, if you need significant funding to achieve your goals, you may need to be willing to give up more equity and control.

Other terms to consider in a venture capital deal include the valuation of your StartUp, the timeline for reaching certain milestones, and the potential for future funding rounds. It's important to work closely with a lawyer and financial advisor to fully understand the terms of any agreement and ensure they align with your Startup's long-term goals and vision.

Negotiating the terms of a deal with venture capitalists can be a complex process. Still, with careful consideration and a clear understanding of potential trade-offs, you can secure funding to help your StartUp grow and thrive.

Post-investment Relationship Management:

Post-investment relationship management is a critical success factor for any StartUp seeking VC funding. Once the transaction is concluded, the relationship between the StartUp and the VC firm enters a new phase. This phase is about managing both parties' expectations, communicating regularly, and ensuring the StartUp is on track to meet its milestones and goals.

One of the most important aspects of post-investment relationship management is maintaining open and transparent communication. This means providing regular updates to the VC firm on the Startup's progress, including any challenges that may arise. It also means being receptive to company feedback and working collaboratively to resolve any issues that may arise.

Another important aspect of post-investment relationship management is staying focused on the goals and milestones set during the initial pitch and negotiation process. It is important to ensure that the StartUp achieves these goals and is on track to achieve the expected return on investment for the venture capitalist.

At the same time, it's also important for the StartUp to keep innovating and pivoting as needed to respond to changing market conditions or to take advantage of new opportunities. This requires maintaining the Startup's original vision and goals while being flexible and responsive to changing circumstances.

Post-investment relationship management requires a proactive approach and ongoing effort from the StartUp and the VC firm. By maintaining open communication, staying focused on goals and milestones, and being flexible and responsive to changing circumstances, StartUps can maximize their chances of success and build strong, lasting relationships with their VC partners.

Benefits and Risks of Venture Capitalists Funding:

Assessing the benefits and risks of working with venture capitalists for your StartUp is crucial for every founder to consider. For one thing, venture capitalists can provide the funding, resources, and expertise needed to accelerate your

Startup's growth and success. They can also offer valuable connections and access to networks that can be difficult to cultivate independently.

However, working with venture capitalists also comes with certain risks and trade-offs. For example, founders may have to give up significant ownership and control of their business in exchange for the investment. There may also be pressure to meet aggressive growth goals and timelines, impacting corporate culture and priorities. Additionally, there may be conflicts of interest between the venture capitalist and the StartUp, particularly if the company has investments in competing businesses or has different priorities than the StartUp.

It's important for founders to carefully weigh the benefits and risks of working with venture capitalists before making a decision. This includes considering their Startup's current stage of development, growth potential, funding needs, and their own goals and priorities for the business. By weighing the pros and cons, founders can make informed decisions aligning with their Startup's vision and mission.

Navigating the Potential Downsides of VC Funding:

VC funding can give StartUps a significant boost in funding, strategic direction, and industry connections. However, it also comes with potential downsides that entrepreneurs should be aware of and navigate cautiously. One of these drawbacks is the loss of control and ownership, as venture capitalists often demand a stake in the business in return for their investment. This can lead to equity dilution, meaning the founders own a smaller percentage of the business.

Another potential downside is the pressure to achieve rapid growth and profitability, which can lead to sacrificing long-term sustainability for short-term gains. This pressure can also lead to a misalignment of goals between the StartUp and its investors, as the latter may prioritize quick returns over the former's vision and mission.

In addition, VC funding may come with certain conditions or requirements that limit the Startup's freedom and flexibility in decision-making. For example, investors can require the StartUp to reach certain milestones or achieve certain growth goals within a specified time frame. This can create additional stress and pressure for the StartUp team and potentially lead to misallocation of resources.

Finally, VC funding can also lead to increased oversight and accountability, as investors will closely monitor the progress and performance of the StartUp. This can be positive and negative, as it can provide valuable feedback and advice and add additional pressure to the StartUp team.

Although VC funding can be a powerful tool for StartUps, it is essential to assess and weigh the potential downsides against the upsides carefully. In addition, entrepreneurs must consider their long-term goals and priorities and their willingness to relinquish control and ownership in exchange for funding and support.

Pitching to venture capitalists can be complex and difficult. Still, it's an essential step for many StartUps looking to secure the necessary funding to grow and scale their business. The promoters need to understand the unique considerations and best practices involved in pitching to venture capitalists, including preparing for the requirements and expectations of a VC pitch, crafting from a compelling pitch deck, building relationships with investors, demonstrating a viable path to return on investment, negotiating terms and conditions, and managing the post-investment relationship.

By following these strategies and considering the potential downsides of VC funding, StartUps can position themselves for success in securing the investment they need to take their business to the next level. While the process can be challenging, the benefits of securing VC funding can be significant, providing StartUps with the resources they need to drive growth, scale their operations, and achieve their long-term goals. Ultimately, the key to success in pitching to venture capitalists is to be prepared, focused, and strategic and to approach the process with a clear understanding of the unique considerations and best practices involved in securing this type of investment.

Negotiating the terms of a deal with venture capitalists can be a complex process. Still, with careful consideration and a clear understanding of potential trade-offs, you can secure funding to help your StartUp grow and thrive.

Post-investment Relationship Management:

Post-investment relationship management is a critical success factor for any StartUp seeking venture capital funding. Once the transaction is concluded, the relationship between the StartUp and the VC firm enters a new phase. This phase is about managing both parties' expectations, communicating regularly, and ensuring the StartUp is on track to meet its milestones and goals.

One of the most important aspects of post-investment relationship management is maintaining open and transparent communication. This means providing regular updates to the VC firm on the Startup's progress, including any challenges that may arise. It also means being receptive to company feedback and working collaboratively to resolve any issues that may arise.

Another important aspect of post-investment relationship management is staying focused on the goals and milestones set during the initial pitch and negotiation process. It is important to ensure that the StartUp achieves these goals and is on track to achieve the expected return on investment for the venture capitalist.

At the same time, it's also important for the StartUp to keep innovating and pivoting as needed to respond to changing market conditions or to take advantage of new opportunities. This requires maintaining the Startup's original vision and goals while being flexible and responsive to changing circumstances.

Post-investment relationship management requires a proactive approach and ongoing effort from the StartUp and the VC firm. By maintaining open communication, staying focused on goals and milestones, and being flexible and responsive to changing circumstances, StartUps can maximize their chances of success and build strong, lasting relationships with their VC partners.

Pitching to venture capitalists can be complex and difficult. Still, it's an essential step for many StartUps looking to secure the necessary funding to grow and scale their business. Therefore, it is important to understand the unique considerations and best practices involved in pitching to venture capitalists, including preparing for the requirements and expectations of a VC pitch, crafting from a compelling pitch deck, building relationships with investors, demonstrating a viable path to return on investment, negotiating terms and conditions, and managing the post-investment relationship.

By following these strategies and considering the potential downsides of VC funding, StartUps can position themselves for success in securing the investment they need to take their business to the next level. While the process can be challenging, the benefits of securing VC funding can be significant, providing StartUps with the resources they need to drive growth, scale their operations, and achieve their long-term goals. Ultimately, the key to success in pitching to venture capitalists is to be prepared, focused, and strategic and to approach the process with a clear understanding of the unique considerations and best practices involved in securing this type of investment.

Chapter 25
Pitching to Private Equity Firms

Unique Considerations and Best Practices

Private equity firms (PE Firms) are investment firms that provide capital to non-publicly listed companies not traded on an exchange, unlike venture capitalists who invest in early-stage businesses with high growth potential. Instead, private equity firms often focus on established businesses with proven results, providing funding options for scale-up operations, market expansion, or merger and acquisition financing.

PE firms requires a different approach than pitching VC firms. PE firms tend to favour companies with established track records of financial performance and an established plan for growth and profitability; they tend to invest in established businesses with proven success records in return for ownership stakes or partial ownership stakes in exchange for their funding.

This chapter will discuss the considerations and best

practices of pitching to PE firms. We will try to understand their role in funding businesses and requirements and expectations when pitching to them, crafting compelling pitches to resonate with investors, and strategies for engaging their attention through presentations that resonate. In addition, we will cover topics such as negotiating deal terms, managing equity considerations, and assessing the benefits/risks of working with them.

Role of Private Equity Firms in Financing:

PE firms have various investment strategies and key components to their business plans. PE firms pool capital from individual and institutional investors to purchase and invest in companies with potentially high returns. PE firms differ from VC firms in that they tend to focus more heavily on more established companies with proven success or significant growth potential than early-stage firms. PE can invest across numerous industries, including healthcare, technology, energy, and manufacturing.

PE firms maintain long-term investment horizons of five to ten years or longer. Over this timeframe, they work closely with the management of companies they invest in to enhance operational efficiencies, expand market share and drive revenue growth. In addition, PE firms may acquire other companies to increase scale and diversify revenue streams.

PE firms employ various investment strategies, including leveraged buyouts (LBOs), growth equity investments, and distressed investing. Leveraged buyouts involve purchasing a company using large amounts of debt financing to improve operations and sell for a profit in the future. Growth equity investments involve investing in companies with proven track records to speed up that growth. At the same time, distressed investing focuses on turning them around to generate returns.

Understanding PE firms' roles and investment strategies is

vital for StartUps and entrepreneurs seeking funding from these entities.

Identify Suitable PE Firms:

Selecting and pitching to the appropriate PE firms is essential to securing funding for your business. PE firms fund non-publicly traded companies to grow and increase returns for companies and their investors.

To find suitable PE firms to pitch to, you must research and understand the type of businesses and industries they usually invest in by reviewing their investment portfolio and what sectors and companies they have previously invested in. Furthermore, it's also vital that you understand their size, the typical size of investments they make, and any criteria or preferences they might have; such information is often found by networking and speaking to industry experts.

When selecting PE firms to pitch, understanding their investment strategy and approach is an important consideration. For example, some PE firms specialize in investing in distressed or turnaround companies, while others target growth-stage firms in specific industries. Knowing their investment approach allows you to craft your pitch appropriately and ensure your business fits their investment goals.

Consideration should also be given to any PE firm's reputation and track record before approaching them. Seek firms with proven expertise, successful investments, and positive relationships with their portfolio companies. A reputable PE firm can bring more than capital; it could offer invaluable industry expertise, connections, and guidance and help your business expand and succeed.

Locating and selecting appropriate PE firms requires extensive research. Learning more about each firm's investment criteria, strategy, and track record increases your odds of securing funding while building long-term partnerships.

Special Requirements and Expectations of PE Pitches:

Preparing to pitch to PE firms involves careful preparations. PE investors often have different investment criteria than venture capitalists or angel investors, tending to favour established companies with proven profitability and growth potential over StartUps that require much more funding, like venture capitalists or angels. Therefore, StartUps looking for funding must demonstrate strong financials, an identifiable growth strategy, and clearly outlined plans for reaching their objectives.

One key element of preparing for a PE pitch is understanding and researching the investment criteria of firms you are targeting, including reviewing past investments, their typical investment sizes and sector preferences, as well as any other relevant details that could allow you to tailor your pitch directly towards their specific needs and preferences.

Preparing for a PE pitch requires crafting an impactful value proposition for your products or services, outlining how they meet specific market needs while setting them apart from competitors. You must also provide an in-depth financial overview, including revenue, profit margins, and other relevant metrics that showcase its financial health and potential growth.

Predict the questions and concerns PE investors might raise about your business by identifying any weaknesses or challenges it might present, along with creating an action plan to deal with them immediately. Doing this increases your chances of successfully securing PE funding.

Pitch Deck for PE Funding:

Understanding their distinct investment criteria and perspectives requires crafting an engaging pitch deck that resonates with PE investors. Since PE firms typically favour established businesses with proven track records of growth and profitability versus VC firms that may invest in early-stage StartUps, your pitch deck should emphasize the company's financial performance, market share, and growth potential.

Your pitch deck should include key financial metrics for your company, such as revenue, EBITDA (Earnings before Interest Taxes Depreciation Amortization), net income projections, and future growth plans. In addition, it should give an overview of your competitive landscape, target market, and strategic initiatives taken to capture market share.

Your pitch deck must also showcase your team's experience and expertise in managing operations and the company's growth. PE firms frequently seek partnerships with businesses that possess strong management teams. You should also be ready to discuss potential business risks or challenges and how you intend to tackle them.

Your pitch deck must clearly and compellingly communicate the value proposition for your business that satisfies the investment criteria and expectations of PE investors. In addition, it should demonstrate your company's ability to generate consistent returns while creating long-term value for its investors.

Demonstrate Proven Growth Potential of Your Business:

When pitching to PE firms, it is vital to demonstrate the growth and profitability of your business. PE investors look for companies with the potential to generate significant returns on investment; they require evidence that shows how your organization plans on doing just this.

Potential for business growth is essential, so provide a clear vision of its future - including long-term goals and how you are going to meet them. Include details regarding target markets, market share capture strategies, and any competitive advantages your business possesses, such as proprietary technologies or an innovative business model.

As well as showing your business can generate growth potential, it should also demonstrate significant profitability. To do so, provide financial projections with clear paths toward profitability as well as discuss any other elements contributing to its financial success. Be ready to discuss revenue models or any other components contributing to its financial success as part of a discussion of your revenue model and any other aspects contributing to financial success in business.

Importantly, PE investors prioritize businesses that have already reached certain levels of success - such as demonstrated revenue and profitability. But even if your business is still in an early stage of growth, demonstrating its potential can still demonstrate profits by emphasizing its business model and providing detailed financial projections using realistic assumptions.

Demonstrating growth and profitability are critical components of pitching to PE firms. By outlining a clear vision for your future and providing specific financial projections, you increase the odds of receiving funding to expand and advance your business to its fullest potential.

Management of Equity and Ownership Considerations in PE Deals:

PE firms invest in companies in exchange for equity ownership, making any deal's equity and ownership considerations central components. In addition, PE firms usually seek a controlling interest in companies they invest in, meaning the founders and management teams may give up some control of the business to these investors.

Establishing the appropriate equity stake when offering your company to a PE firm is of utmost importance in maintaining founder and management team ownership and control. The equity structure can vary based on factors such as the investment size, stage of business development, and risk profile of the investment.

Some PE firms require investments to be structured as preferred equity or convertible debt investments, which could have serious ramifications on your equity and ownership considerations. Therefore, before discussing with PE firms, the promoters must understand any possible impacts of getting PE investment.

PE firms often require the implementation of an equity incentive plan for management and employees. This plan allows management and employees to share in the business's success while incentivizing them to reach its goals.

Equity and ownership considerations in PE deals require careful thought and negotiation to reach an agreement that benefits both the firm investing and the target company's founders and management team.

Different Kinds of PE Deals and Structures:

PE deals and structures come in various forms, so you must learn each type to identify which best suits your business. However, here are some common forms of PE transactions and structures:

Leveraged Buyouts (LBOs): With this type of PE deal, a PE firm acquires control of an established company using significant debt financing. The transaction aims to improve profits while creating shareholder value by cutting costs and expanding revenues. LBOs work well when applied to established businesses with steady cash flows that require significant improvements.

Growth Capital: Growth capital investments involve PE firms investing in companies that have already established their business model and seek to expand. These deals are less risky than LBOs, providing the capital required for expanding and increasing the business value.

Venture Capital: VC deals typically involve investments in early-stage companies with high growth potential to fund product development, expand operations and attract top talent. Though high risk, VC investments can produce substantial returns.

Mezzanine Financing: Mezzanine financing provides debt capital to companies seeking expansion. Mezzanine investors typically rank lower on priority than senior debt holders but higher than equity holders when providing capital.

Distressed Debt: PE firms investing in distressed debt deals typically target companies experiencing financial distress to restructure and return them to profitability, providing potential returns that may exceed any initial risks involved. However, such investments may involve high risks and considerable potential returns.

Understanding the different types of PE deals and structures can help you select the most suitable one for your business. Each option has its advantages and risks; to make an informed decision, the investee company needs to compare potential benefits and drawbacks and make an informed decision based on solid facts.

Negotiating and Structuring Deals to Maximize Value:

Negotiating deal terms and structuring the deal to maximize value for both parties involved is integral to pitching to PE firms. Once you have selected an ideal firm to approach and constructed an engaging pitch deck, the next step should be negotiating the terms of the deal.

At this stage, it is critical to recognize that negotiation can be complex and time-consuming. The process requires carefully considering various aspects such as the valuation of your business, terms of the investment agreement, and level of control you retain over the partnership, and expected return on investment.

Take an open approach to maximize value for both parties involved in negotiations. Accept feedback and suggestions from the PE firm as they arise and be willing to compromise on certain terms in exchange for favourable terms on other points.

One of the primary factors in structuring any deal involves selecting an investment type for a PE firm to make. PE deals may take various forms, including leveraged buyouts, growth equity funding, mezzanine financing, or distressed debt investments - each type has different risks and rewards associated with it before finalizing a deal is signed off on.

Structure the deal so you retain maximum control over its strategic direction and business activities. Although PE firms tend to want more say over companies they invest in, it is still possible to negotiate terms that allow you to keep some control over the strategic direction of your company. Companies should also carefully consider an investment's terms, including its debt level, interest rate, and expected return. Negotiating favourable terms for these factors will increase the chance that the venture will succeed and position your business for long-term growth.

Negotiating terms and structuring deals to maximize value requires an in-depth knowledge of the investment landscape, an open dialogue approach to negotiation, and a willingness to sacrifice some terms in exchange for favourable terms on other aspects.

Due Diligence Process with PE investors:

Due diligence is an integral component of PE investment. It involves an intensive analysis by the PE firm into your business to assess its risks and opportunities associated with investing. To evaluate risk, due diligence involves reviewing various aspects of your organization, such as finances, operations, legal compliance, and management structure. Therefore, preparation is key to ensuring an efficient due diligence process that does not delay an investment deal.

As part of your preparation for due diligence, it is essential to have all financial and operational documents ready, including financial statements, tax returns, contracts, and employee records. In addition, be prepared to give extensive details on your business model, marketing strategy, sales channels, and customer base. Finally, identify any red flags that may arise during due diligence and devise a plan to address them if necessary.

During due diligence, remaining open and cooperative with a PE firm is essential. Be ready to answer their queries promptly and promptly provide any additional information they request. In addition, have a clear understanding of the due diligence timeline so all parties involved adhere to it.

Due diligence can be intricate and complex for those unfamiliar with PE investments. In addition, it can often prove more challenging if they lack experience managing this aspect of investments themselves. Therefore, hiring an experienced advisor or attorney could prove helpful in managing it more efficiently; they could assist with gathering all required documents, identifying any potential issues, and helping your company connect with its target PE firm more easily.

Due diligence can be time-consuming and complicated;

however, it's an integral component of PE investment. Being prepared and cooperative throughout can ensure a smooth process and increase the chance of a successful investment decision.

Risks and Benefits Associated with PE Funding:

PE firms are investment funds that invest in privately held companies with the aim of producing a return for their investors. Partnering with a PE firm may bring many advantages for businesses, such as accessing capital, expertise and experience, and strategic guidance. However, there may also be potential risks and drawbacks that should be carefully considered before entering into any agreement with one.

One of the advantages of PE is access to capital. PE firms generally invest large sums of money in companies, providing an invaluable boost in growth and expansion plans. This money could fund research and development activities, expand into new markets, or purchase other businesses - to name a few potential uses.

PE firms also provide expertise and experience to the businesses they invest in, which is especially valuable for smaller enterprises that may lack the resources or skills needed to take advantage of growth opportunities on their own. They may guide strategy, operations, and management, as well as access to their network of contacts and resources.

Working with a PE firm could bring many potential advantages, including an IPO or acquisition event that provides significant returns to shareholders of your business. In addition, PE firms usually have set timeframes for their investments and strive to maximize value before exiting an investment from their portfolio companies.

But PE firms come with their own set of risks and drawbacks, which you should keep in mind before signing on with one. One such risk is loss of control: these investors often require significant equity stakes in companies they invest in, diluting ownership and control held by founders and management teams. Furthermore, different priorities or goals may cause conflicts.

Pressure to achieve quick returns can also pose a danger. PE firms focus on getting quick returns for their investments, which can create pressure to cut costs or increase revenue that might not serve the long-term viability of businesses in highly competitive industries or rapidly evolving sectors. This may put long-term viability at stake as short-term gains come at the cost of long-term viability.

The final consideration should include costs associated with working with a PE firm. For example, PE firms tend to charge management fees. In addition, they may demand a portion of profits generated by investments they manage, so these costs must be thoroughly considered before entering an agreement with any PE firm.

Working with a PE firm can bring many advantages for any business, but it's essential to carefully weigh any possible risks or drawbacks before entering an agreement with one. By understanding both, businesses can make informed decisions as to whether engaging with such firms is appropriate for their needs.

PE firms are investment funds that invest in privately held companies to produce a return for their investors. Working with a PE firm may bring many advantages for your business, including access to capital, expertise, experience, and strategic guidance. Still, it would help if you considered any risks or drawbacks before entering into such an agreement.

Working with a PE firm may bring you access to capital. Such firms typically invest significant sums of money into businesses, significantly boosting growth and expansion plans. With access to this capital, your company could use it for research and development funding, expanding into new markets, or even acquiring other businesses - among many other uses.

PE firms provide businesses they invest in with capital, expertise, and experience, which is particularly helpful to smaller firms that lack the resources or expertise needed to take advantage of growth opportunities. In addition, PE firms may guide in areas like strategy, operations management, and management, as well as access to their contacts and resources.

PE firms seek a promise of an exit event, such as an initial public offering (IPO) or acquisition that can provide significant returns for founders and other shareholders of your company. PE firms usually follow an investment timeline and strive to maximize the value of portfolio companies before exiting them, making a partnership more likely.

However, PE has its own risks and drawbacks to consider. One such risk is control. PE firms require significant equity stakes in companies they invest in, which dilutes ownership and control held by founders and management teams. Furthermore, different priorities or goals may lead to conflicts with these investors.

Pressure to produce short-term results is another significant threat PE firm's pose. Their focus on quick returns often requires them to cut costs or increase revenue in ways that might not serve the long-term interests of their investments; this can be especially difficult in sectors with highly competitive or rapidly shifting industries, where short-term gains might come at the cost of long-term viability.

Finally, it is essential to carefully consider the potential costs associated with working with a PE firm. They often charge management fees and take a share of profits from investments. It is wise to carefully assess these potential costs before entering into any agreements with PE firms.

Cooperating with a PE firm can bring many advantages to a business. Yet, businesses must consider all potential risks and rewards before entering into an agreement with one. By understanding PE firms' potential benefits and drawbacks, businesses can make informed decisions regarding whether working with one meets their specific requirements.

Manage relationships with PE investors:

Managing post-investment relationships is important to successful working relationships with PE investors. Once an investment is secured, regular communication should take place between you and them to provide updates on business performance and address any concerns they might have - this helps build trust and create positive associations between both parties involved.

PE firms usually expect a high degree of involvement in the management of businesses they invest in after investing and may appoint someone to sit on your board of directors or participate in decision-making processes. Therefore, establishing clear lines of communication and roles and responsibilities between your business and PE firms is essential to ensure clarity and understanding between the parties involved.

PE firms focus on producing returns for their investors and typically set an exit strategy within several years, whether through sale, IPO, or other means. Therefore, an exit strategy that works toward that end goal and working with your PE firm toward it must be in place.

Sometimes, PE firms provide additional resources or expertise that help drive growth and improve performance, such as operational or financial restructuring. It's important to remain open-minded regarding these possibilities and collaborate with your PE firm to achieve desired results.

Managing post-investment relationships with PE investors requires open communication, clear expectations and roles, and an emphasis on generating returns and meeting exit strategies agreed upon between all parties involved. As a result, businesses can take advantage of PE firms' expertise while increasing value creation among all involved.

Pitching to PE Firms:

Pitching to PE firms requires different considerations and best practices compared to VC firms. PE firms like to invest in more mature businesses with proven profitability or substantial potential for growth. Entrepreneurs seeking PE funding must research the right PE firms they wish to pitch to; prepare an engaging pitch deck that showcases their value proposition; negotiate deal terms that maximize value creation for both parties involved; negotiate terms that maximize returns for both.

Considerations should also be given to equity and ownership issues, preparation for due diligence, potential downsides of PE funding, and how best to maintain relationships post-investment. Hence, the business continues its expansion and success.

PE funding offers several significant advantages to entrepreneurs, including access to capital, expertise, and resources. But entrepreneurs must carefully consider its potential drawbacks: loss of control and flexibility, increased accountability, and potential conflicts of interest - before considering PE funding as a useful solution for expanding their businesses further. Nevertheless, with careful thought and strategic application, PE funding can become invaluable for taking your company forward.

◆◆◆

Chapter 26
Demystifying Angel Investing

What Angel Investors Look for in a Pitch?

Angel investing has become an increasingly popular source of StartUp funding, with angel investors providing early-stage capital in exchange for equity stakes in promising StartUps. But entrepreneurs often find pitching to angel investors daunting and daunting; to effectively secure funding through angel investing, entrepreneurs must understand what angel investors look for when pitching them and learn how to communicate their business ideas to them effectively.

This chapter will demystify angel investing and provide entrepreneurs with insight into what angel investors expect in a pitch. We'll also examine special considerations and best practices when pitching to angel investors, such as researching and identifying prospective investors, developing an engaging pitch deck, navigating due diligence procedures, and managing post-investment relationships effectively.

Understanding Angel Investors in StartUp Funding:

Angel investors are high-net-worth individuals who invest personal funds into early-stage StartUps for equity ownership in exchange for personal funds invested. Angels typically prefer companies too risky or early-stage for traditional VC firms or other types of investors, such as PE firms or institutional investors, to fund.

Angel investors are the "first line of defence" when StartUps need funding. Angels may provide seed capital or follow-on funding as StartUps start up or grow and scale. Angel investors also provide valuable expertise, mentorship, and connections to other investors and industry experts that StartUps rely on.

Angel investors play a vital role in the StartUp ecosystem, often being the first investors to recognize the potential of new ideas or technologies. In addition, their involvement can help StartUps navigate through what is known as the "valley of death," where funding becomes limited. In contrast, risks become high during the early development stages of a company's evolution.

StartUps often rely on angel investors as an invaluable source of funding and support, enabling them to turn their ideas into viable businesses. To secure funding effectively from angel investors, however, StartUps must understand their expectations and preferences to pitch their businesses and secure funding.

Identification of StartUps that Interest Angel Investors:

For entrepreneurs looking for angel investment, understanding which types of StartUps interest angel investors are an integral step. Angels tend to favour fast-growth StartUps that could produce significant returns. However, angels also appreciate innovative concepts with disruptive business models and new approaches for solving established industry issues.

Angel investors prefer StartUps with an apparent market opportunity and target audience in mind, which demonstrate demand for their product or service and have a viable plan to capture a share of that market. Entrepreneurs focused on solving an unrecognized need in the market may particularly attract angel investment dollars.

Angel investors tend to favour StartUps with strong founding teams with complementary skills and experiences who possess all of the expertise required to execute a business plan, with proven successes in previous ventures. In addition, Angel investors may especially find appealing StartUps with an engaging narrative about their founding team members' vision for the future and its development.

Angel investors look for StartUps with a clear plan for generating revenue and reaching profitability, such as evidence of their business model being well-defined with sustainable growth in mind. In addition, StartUps that demonstrate that they have carefully considered revenue streams, pricing strategy, and cost structures may be particularly appealing to angel investors.

Search and Identification of Angel Investors for Pitching: Conducting thorough research on and identifying suitable angel investors to pitch to is a crucial component of fundraising, not only providing capital but also offering expertise, networks, mentorship, and mentorship benefits for your StartUp. Therefore you must conduct extensive due diligence on and identify angel investors who share your industry, goals, and visions.

One effective method for finding angel investors is online research. Websites like Angel List, Gust, and Seed Invest provide databases of angel investors, including their investment preferences and previous investments. Entrepreneurs may also leverage social media platforms like LinkedIn or Twitter to connect with potential investors.

Another effective strategy for finding angel investors is through networking events and conferences. Attending industry-related gatherings offers you an excellent chance to meet investors who share an interest in your field; additionally, these conferences allow you to hear more about their experiences and understand what they look for when considering potential StartUps for funding.

Entrepreneurs can leverage their network, including colleagues, mentors, advisors, and fellow entrepreneurs, for referrals of angel investors with successful track records who may be interested in StartUps similar to your own. Referrals can be an effective way to find potential angel investors with similar investment interests and may provide invaluable leads that lead them directly to potential angel investments.

Having compiled an initial list of potential angel investors, entrepreneurs should research each investor to understand better their investment preferences, portfolio companies, and track record. This knowledge can assist entrepreneurs in customizing their pitch to each investor based on their specific interests and expertise.

Researching and identifying suitable angel investors to pitch to, is a vital step in the fundraising process. By searching for potential angel investors through online research, networking events, referrals, and potential investor research tools such as Angel List or Crunch base, entrepreneurs can quickly find investors that can take their StartUp forward.

Establish a clear and compelling elevator pitch that accurately summarizes your StartUp.

Preparing an elevator pitch that captures the essence of your business and communicates its value proposition clearly and succinctly is of great importance when approaching angel investors. Therefore, an elevator pitch should be a short, engaging message summarizing its key aspects concisely and convincingly.

To craft an effective elevator pitch, identify your target audience and their needs. Next, consider what makes your StartUp unique while addressing its pain points, and finally, condense all this information into several memorable bullet points that are easy to communicate and remember.

When crafting your elevator pitch, it is key to emphasize the benefits rather than the features of your StartUp. Point out how your solution addresses a particular problem and highlight its positive impacts on society and life. Also, ensure that it reflects who you are as an organization and its core values.

Be confident and engaging when giving your elevator pitch, and be willing to adjust it based on feedback received. Finally, remember that an elevator pitch is just the start of any conversation with angel investors; be prepared to provide additional details and answer any questions they might pose after hearing it.

An impressive elevator pitch can help captivate angel investors and generate interest in your StartUp. A successful pitch should pique their curiosity and convince them to explore further about your venture.

Crafting a Pitch Deck That Engages Angel Investors: Crafting a pitch deck that resonates with angel investors is crucial in winning their investment for your StartUp. Angel investors receive many pitches every week, looking for new and promising opportunities; your pitch deck must grab their attention immediately and hold it throughout.

First, your pitch deck must be clear, concise, and well-structured. Include information on your business, such as a summary, market analysis, competitive landscape assessment, financial projections, management team, unique value proposition, and what sets your StartUp apart.

Design of Your Pitch:

The design of your pitch deck should also be key - it should be visually appealing with a consistent colour scheme and font, without too much text cluttering up its slides. In addition, images or graphs should help make your presentation more engaging!

When creating your pitch deck, it's essential to remember what angel investors expect of it. They want a comprehensive business plan demonstrating growth potential and profitability and an experienced management team with proven success records.

Your pitch deck should present an engaging narrative about your StartUp and why it represents an attractive investment opportunity. By crafting an eye-catching pitch deck that effectively presents this story to potential angel investors, your chances of receiving funding increase substantially.

Demonstrating an attractive Return of Investment Path for Angel Investors: Establishing a viable path to return on investment for angel investors is a key aspect of any pitch. They tend to favour high-growth StartUps that could provide significant returns quickly on their investments, so it's essential that your StartUp clearly communicate how its future value creation and revenue generation will take place.

To demonstrate a path toward ROI, you must present a detailed business plan which includes financial projections, market analysis, and growth strategies. This will allow angel investors to evaluate your business potential while understanding the risks and opportunities involved.

Your business plan should also contain an exit strategy that outlines how angel investors can cash out their investment, such as selling the company, going public through an IPO, or buying out by another larger firm.

As part of your Startup's business plan, it's also crucial to provide evidence of its traction and validation - such as customer testimonials, market research data, or revenue forecasts based on existing sales.

As part of your efforts to secure investment from angel investors, demonstrating an achievable path to ROI is critical. By providing a comprehensive business plan with evidence of traction and an exit strategy for your StartUp venture, you can show them that it could yield significant returns for their money.

Dealing with Equity and Ownership Considerations in Angel Investment Deals:

Proper management of equity and ownership considerations in angel investment deals is of utmost importance when raising funds from angel investors. While VC firms may seek substantial equity stakes for significant funding, angel investors tend to be more flexible with structuring their investments - and may accept other forms of investments beyond equity as part of the agreement.

Considerations should also be given to whether offering preferred shares, which would grant angel investors additional rights and privileges over common shareholders, will increase the return on investment for angel investment. StartUps should prepare to negotiate with angel investors to determine an acceptable equity stake that strikes a balance between return on investment for angels and maintaining control of their business for founders.

Another key consideration for StartUps should be how angel investors impact the ownership structure. For example,

StartUps may wish to implement a vesting schedule for founders and early employees so that everyone has the incentive to stay with the company over time and contribute towards its development - this may help prevent conflicts arising should an angel investor require changes to be made regarding ownership structure.

Finally, StartUps should be mindful of any dilution of ownership arising from additional investment. Founders must negotiate carefully to protect key decisions from being ceded away for funding - including potential anti-dilution clauses to safeguard against further rounds.

Equity and ownership considerations are central to any successful angel investment deal. StartUps should prepare to negotiate with angel investors to receive an equitable stake in their investment while still maintaining control of their business and protecting existing shareholders' interests.

Negotiating and Closing Deals with Angel Investors:

Negotiating term sheets and closing deals with angel investors are integral to raising capital for your StartUp. Once you've identified potential angel investors and developed an engaging pitch that resonates with them, the next step should be negotiating a term sheet outlining all key terms of their investment agreement.

A term sheet is a document that contains the basic terms of an investment agreement. This typically includes information like the amount invested, valuation of the company, percentage of equity sold off to investors, and their rights and protections. A term sheet is a starting point for negotiations between entrepreneurs and angel investors.

Negotiating the term sheet requires consideration of its long-term ramifications, including potential effects on company equity structure and ownership, future financing rounds, and possible tax implications.

Negotiate terms that are fair and reasonable for both parties involved. Angel investors typically seek returns on their investment; therefore, it's essential to demonstrate how this investment will lead to growth and profitability for the business.

Once the term sheet has been agreed upon, the next step should be to finalize and close the deal and investment. This includes creating legal documents such as investment and shareholder agreements and ensuring all parties understand its terms and conditions.

Claiming an investment from angel investors is an exciting momentous step for any StartUp, yet it must be remembered that relationships between StartUps and angel investors continue. Therefore, maintain open and transparent communication with these investors and update them on your company's growth.

Understanding the different stages of angel investing, as well as what investors look for at each phase:

Angel investing often happens in stages, with each phase having different investment requirements and expectations. Understanding these phases and what investors look for at each point is the key to successfully raising funds from angel investors.

The earliest stage of angel investing is the Seed Stage. Currently, StartUps with only prototypes or minimum viable products (MVP) may seek funds to develop further and assemble their team and product offering. Angel investors at this stage require strong teams with experienced personnel capable of carrying out their business plans, clearly defined market opportunities, and an obvious path toward revenue generation as criteria for investment consideration.

At this early stage, angel investors look for StartUps with products or services generating some revenue but require additional funds to expand. Here, angel investors look for evidence of market traction and an efficient go-to-market strategy; additionally, they will assess any plans to scale the Startup's operations.

At this stage, investors seek evidence of sustainable growth with a plan for profitability; additionally, they prefer StartUps with experienced management, strong market position, and plans to enter new markets.

The exit stage refers to when a StartUp is sold, merged, or taken public. Angel investors want to see that their investment has produced value while offering clear exit strategies for their investments.

Understanding these stages of angel investing is crucial for StartUps seeking funding from angel investors. By tailoring their pitch to each stage, StartUps can more successfully meet investor expectations and improve their chances of securing funds.

Navigating the Potential Drawbacks of Angel Investment: Angel investment can be an appealing source of StartUp funding due to its promise of high returns and flexible terms of investment. But entrepreneurs should also be wary of working with angel investors due to possible drawbacks - one being that angel investors may exert too much control over your company in exchange for their investment - via board seats, decision-making authority, or other forms of control that they exert over you in return.

Angel investors may have different expectations from traditional venture capitalists or other investors, placing greater weight on short-term gains rather than long-term growth and sustainability of a company. This can put undue pressure on entrepreneurs seeking quick wins while neglecting the long-term prospects of their investment.

Angel investors present another potential drawback when working together in the form of conflicts of interest. For example, Angel investors could hold investments in competing or related companies that could present conflicts that damage a company's prospects; similarly, an angel investor who becomes dissatisfied with your progress might seek to sell off their stake and cause disruption or harm its reputation.

Entrepreneurs should also be mindful that angel investment carries dilution risks and loss of control. As the company secures additional funding rounds, existing investors may see their ownership stakes reduced over time, potentially diminishing their influence and control over the company. Furthermore, they risk losing its investment entirely if it fails to meet its goals or faces other difficulties.

Angel investment can be an excellent source of StartUp funding; however, entrepreneurs should consider any possible risks or downsides and consider any agreements between angel investors and StartUps. By understanding both risks and benefits associated with working with angel investors, entrepreneurs can make informed decisions to maximize long-term success.

Maintaining positive and productive relations with angel investors:

Angel investors play a vital role in any Startup's success; not only do they offer funding, but they bring invaluable industry expertise, experience, and connections that should not be disregarded once the deal has closed. Therefore, post-investment relationships between StartUps and angel investors must be positive and beneficial, even after investment agreements have been finalized.

One key to managing post-investment relationships with angel investors is maintaining regular dialogue. StartUps should provide regular updates on their progress and keep investors abreast of any significant developments or challenges, helping build trust with investors while giving StartUps expert feedback and guidance from experienced professionals.

Another key aspect is transparency. StartUps should always be honest with angel investors about any challenges or changes to their business strategies that they are encountering or any important decisions made, which helps build trust between both parties involved and keeps investors up-to-date with important details.

StartUps must also listen closely to advice and feedback from angel investors since angel investors possess extensive industry expertise that could prove invaluable for StartUps. StartUps should welcome constructive criticism and suggestions from angel investors as feedback, using it to make more informed decisions regarding their business strategies.

StartUps must strive to maintain positive and productive relationships with their angel investors, which includes being responsive to inquiries, providing timely updates, and showing appreciation for their support and contributions. By building such strong and positive bonds with angel investors, StartUps can ensure they have someone on their side as they navigate the ups and downs of StartUp life.

Evaluating the advantages and risks of working with angel investors:

Evaluating the benefits and risks of working with angel investors for your StartUp is an integral component of the funding search. Angel investors offer more than just money - they provide expertise, knowledge, network connections, and credibility benefits, which can assist StartUps when seeking subsequent funding rounds.

Working with angel investors comes with its own set of risks. Most angel investors expect a return on their investment, which may lead to conflicts if their goals don't align. Furthermore, angel investors may have different expectations regarding growth trajectory, exit strategy, and overall direction that could cause tension if not discussed earlier.

Before seeking funding from angel investors, StartUp founders must carefully assess the benefits and risks of working with angel investors. This involves conducting an in-depth investigation on potential investors; conducting due diligence research; learning their investment history and philosophy; and carefully negotiating terms to align goals and expectations. By considering all angles, StartUp founders can make informed decisions regarding which funding sources will provide their companies with optimal returns.

Angel investment can be an important funding source for StartUps, yet it can be daunting to entrepreneurs new to this space. Understanding what angel investors look for in a pitch and constructing an engaging presentation are the keys to successfully raising funds through angel investments. StartUps should develop a concise elevator pitch that captures their business essence before creating a pitch deck that resonates with angel investors; additionally, they need to demonstrate viable paths toward return on investment, manage equity and ownership considerations, and negotiate term sheets before concluding the post-investment relationship successfully.

Angel investment may seem attractive for StartUps, but it is essential to carefully weigh its benefits and risks before deciding if this path suits them. For example, Angel investors may provide funding, invaluable advice, mentorship, connections, influence over company decisions, and time-consuming fundraising processes, taking time away from more important aspects of running a StartUp business.

Decisions on whether or not to partner with angel investors must be carefully made after considering all aspects of their Startup's needs and goals and understanding the process and expectations of angel investors. By being aware of both, entrepreneurs can better position themselves for success in this competitive world of StartUp funding.

Chapter 27
Negotiation Skills Essential to Securing Funding

Here's Where Things Get Interesting

Negotiating effectively is a necessary skill for entrepreneurs seeking funding for their businesses. Negotiation means creating a balance of give and take between the parties involved in a deal. Both parties strive to meet their desired outcomes by negotiating favourable deal terms from investors to obtain the funds they require for growth.

Negotiation is often considered an art form, requiring careful preparation, strategic thinking, and effective communication skills to negotiate funding deals for their businesses successfully. Entrepreneurs with excellent negotiating skills are better equipped to navigate the complexities associated with funding arrangements while creating outcomes that benefit both themselves and their investors. In this chapter, we will present essential tips for effectively negotiating with investors to secure funds for your business as well as discuss common pitfalls to avoid and strategies for reaching positive results.

Understanding the Basics of Deal Negotiation:

Negotiation skills are vitally important for entrepreneurs seeking funding for their business, whether through debt financing or equity investors. Negotiation is a complex process requiring skill and finesse from all parties involved - at its core. It means reaching an agreement acceptable to all involved. In fundraising, this may mean finding common ground on key terms like valuation, ownership, and control with investors.

One of the key principles of negotiation is understanding "BATNA," or Best Alternative to a Negotiated Agreement. This refers to the idea that before entering negotiations, each party should clearly understand their alternatives to any proposed deal; this could include investigating other sources of funding or delaying fundraising processes, or even adopting different business strategies altogether. By having a solid BATNA in mind, entrepreneurs are better placed to negotiate from a position of strength.

Anchoring, or setting initial negotiation terms, is another essential tactic of successful negotiations. Anchoring involves proposing terms that favour your position while remaining within reason - this first offer can greatly affect how things turn out! Therefore, carefully consider your initial terms when crafting proposals and requesting funding.

Other key negotiation principles include:
- Understanding the significance of active listening.
- Framing issues in different ways.
- Building rapport with your negotiating partner.

By mastering these fundamental practices of negotiations, entrepreneurs can increase their chances of creating deals that benefit all parties involved.

Understanding Different Negotiation Styles and Adopting Them:

Everyone approaches negotiations differently, with three general negotiation styles emerging: Competitive, Collaborative, and Compromise.

1. Competitive negotiators often see negotiations as a race to the finish, where only one party will emerge victorious. As a result, they tend to be aggressive and assertive during negotiations and may employ techniques such as bluffing and intimidation to get what they want.

2. Conversely, collaborative negotiators view negotiations as a win-win scenario that benefits both parties involved. They typically involve themselves in collaborative communication efforts while striving for mutual understanding and respect during negotiations.

3. Compromising negotiators represent a middle ground between competitive and collaborative styles of negotiation, making concessions to find an agreement. They're most often utilized when stakes are high, and both parties have equal investment in the outcome of negotiations.

Understanding different negotiation styles is essential, as this knowledge allows you to tailor your approach according to that of the other party. For instance, when dealing with competitive negotiators, you may need to be more assertive and firm with your demands; conversely, if working with collaborative negotiators who tend towards collaboration, you should focus on building rapport and finding common ground instead.

Adopting various negotiation styles can help build trust and rapport, leading to a successful negotiation. Furthermore, knowing your negotiation style's strengths and weaknesses is key to creating an effective strategy.

Setting Realistic Expectations and Goals:

Realistic expectations and goals are an integral component of negotiations. Before entering negotiations, you must fully grasp what you wish to accomplish and where your compromise points lie. In addition, setting expectations that match business goals and financial needs is essential in successfully concluding deals.

To set realistic expectations and goals, begin by conducting thorough market and competition research. This will enable you to assess what is reasonable and achievable when it comes to funding, valuation, and deal terms. It is also essential to consider both your business strengths and weaknesses and any long-term goals when setting expectations and goals.

When setting goals, consider both your business's short- and long-term needs. While securing funding may be essential to its short-term success, be wary that any terms of any deals don't impede long-term growth and profitability.

Setting realistic expectations and goals involves being flexible and open to negotiation. While having a firm grasp on your desired outcomes is key, being willing to listen to other parties needs and concerns may help find common ground and reach mutually beneficial agreements more quickly.

Establishing realistic expectations and goals is the cornerstone of deal negotiation. Conducting extensive research, considering both your short-term and long-term needs, and remaining flexible and open-minded can set up an efficient negotiation process.

Prioritizing Your Negotiations Points:

Negotiation is about understanding what you want out of a deal while being open-minded enough to compromise. Therefore, before entering into negotiations, it is crucial to identify and prioritize your key negotiation points based on importance - this often includes funding amounts, equity ownership percentages, board representation rights, and exit strategies, among other key areas.

Consideration should also be given to how negotiation points look from the other party's point of view and any areas where there may be overlap or common ground to identify potential areas of compromise and increase the chances of reaching an amicable agreement.

Prioritizing your negotiation points is necessary to set realistic expectations and be willing to compromise when necessary. Although you might only be able to reach some of your negotiation goals, recognizing which ones are most essential can be rewarding when combined with willing compromise on other areas to meet them.

Identification and prioritizing negotiation points is a vital element of the negotiation process and will ensure you can secure funding on terms favourable to your business. Strategies for handling difficult negotiations or difficult personalities:

Negotiations can become challenging when both parties hold strong opinions or hold different perspectives about certain aspects of a deal. In addition, you may encounter difficult negotiators who refuse to compromise or intentionally create obstacles during negotiations; when faced with such personalities, you must remain calm, professional, and focused on your negotiation points.

One approach for successfully handling difficult negotiations is taking a collaborative approach. Instead of viewing negotiation as a battle, attempt to find areas of mutual agreement and work towards finding solutions that benefit both sides. Doing this can build trust and rapport - two essential ingredients for securing successful deals.

Stay focused on your priorities and negotiation points to achieve maximum effectiveness during negotiations. While it can be easy to become distracted or defensive when facing difficult personalities, staying true to what you want to achieve with this negotiation may require taking a break or hiring an outside mediator to facilitate discussion.

Be mindful of how others perceive your communication style and try not to be aggressive or confrontational; that could make negotiations more challenging. Instead, aim for assertive communication without being overbearing and focus on finding mutually beneficial solutions rather than "winning" negotiations.

Finally, it's essential that you're prepared to walk away from a negotiation if it is no longer in your best interests. Sometimes a deal isn't realistic or worth the resources necessary for its acquisition; when this occurs, it may be wiser to cut losses and move on to other opportunities.

Techniques for Effectively Controlling Emotions and Maintaining a Professional Demeanour during Negotiations:

Effective deal negotiations require not only a strategic approach but also emotional intelligence. Emotions may run high during negotiations, making it crucial that they are managed appropriately to maintain a professional demeanour and prevent any potential damage to the deal.

One effective technique for controlling emotions during negotiations is practicing active listening. Active listening involves paying close attention to both spoken words and the body language of both parties to understand their perspective better; this strategy can help reduce misunderstandings and enhance communication during negotiations.

Another tactic is to separate people and problems. It is essential to remember that negotiations are about deals, not people involved. By keeping the focus on the problem at hand, negotiators can avoid becoming emotionally invested in negotiations while keeping emotions under control.

Breaks during negotiations can also help manage emotions effectively. For example, taking a short step away from the table for just a moment, taking time out for reflection or relaxation, and then coming back with fresh eyes allow you to return with a clearer mind and make better decisions when returning to the negotiating table.

Finally, negotiators should remain aware of how their emotions might impact negotiations. Enhancing self-awareness helps avoid emotional outbursts or hasty decisions that could compromise deals.

Managing emotions during negotiations requires self-awareness, active listening, and being able to disentangle people from problems. By employing these techniques, negotiators can maintain a professional demeanour while increasing the odds of reaching successful deals.

Establish Your BATNA (Best Alternative To a Negotiated Agreement):

"BATNA" refers to "Best Alternative to a Negotiated Agreement" and your potential options if a negotiation fails and an agreement cannot be reached with another party. Having a clear idea of your BATNA options can help guide strategic decision-making and set achievable goals during any negotiation.

Establishing your Best Alternative to Negotiated Agreement (BATNA) involves evaluating each alternative based on feasibility, desirability, and risk. For example, if you're in negotiations with potential investors, BATNA could include seeking funding from angel investors, venture capitalists, or bank loans as an alternative funding source; or you might consider delaying fundraising efforts altogether or scaling back business plans as other possible measures; alternative options could even include seeking partnerships or collaborations with other businesses.

When developing your BATNA, you must remain objective. Consider all potential risks and benefits of each alternative, its likelihood of success, and any impact this decision might have on your business and future goals.

Understanding your Best Alternative to Negotiated Agreement can assist in more successful negotiations, providing leverage and bargaining power. For example, a strong BATNA may prompt more drastic actions like walking away from a negotiation if it does not favour you. Conversely, a weak BATNA may force concessions or compromises to reach an agreement.

Creating your BATNA is an integral component of negotiations as it can assist you with making informed decisions and setting realistic goals. By exploring various alternatives and understanding them better, you can negotiate more effectively to achieve the best result for your business.

Researching and Understanding your Negotiating Opponent:

Studying and understanding your negotiation counterpart is an integral component of successful deal-making. Before engaging in discussions with another party, it's vital to research their goals, values, and priorities to craft your negotiation plan to fit their specific requirements and desires.

One way to research your negotiation counterpart is by conducting a comprehensive background check. This may involve investigating their company history, financials, and previous deals they have completed and gathering details about their personal history and values.

As well as conducting research, forming relationships with your negotiating counterparts is essential. Establishing rapport and trust can create a more productive negotiating environment and may ultimately lead to greater success for all involved. This may mean finding common ground and goals while being willing to listen and understand other viewpoints.

Remember that both parties are likely doing research and preparing for negotiations, so conducting your own investigation and understanding their perspective can increase your chances of reaching an amicable agreement.

Establishing rapport and building trust are crucial parts of the negotiation. When seeking funding for your business, building strong relationships with both parties is vital to establish trust and create a productive atmosphere to negotiate.

To build rapport, you must focus on connecting with the other party. This may mean finding common interests or experiences you share; conversely, small talk is another effective means of showing that you care about them as individuals rather than just as business partners.

Trust building is another crucial aspect of negotiation. You want the other party to believe you have their best interests in mind and trust you as knowledgeable and reliable; this may involve being open about your goals and intentions and reliable in keeping commitments made during negotiations.

One effective strategy for building rapport and fostering trust during negotiations is conducting thorough research on your counterpart before beginning negotiations. This may involve investigating their history, understanding their values and goals, as well as gathering details about past experiences. Doing this research will enable you to identify areas where there may be common ground as well as demonstrate that you've put forth effort into understanding them better.

As you negotiate, it is crucial to maintain a positive attitude and focus on the shared goals and interests. Doing this can create an atmosphere of partnership and collaboration, making reaching an amicable agreement much simpler.

Negotiations: Balancing Short and Long-term Gains

Successful negotiations involve more than simply seeking out the best outcome for oneself; it also involves building and maintaining relationships. Although striving for favourable short-term results is essential, long-term implications must also be carefully considered. Any bad deal could erode relationships between negotiating parties; any perceived unfair deals could damage those relationships further and potentially damage long-term repercussions.

For long-term gains and relationships to survive, negotiations must be approached with cooperation and mutual benefit. This means focusing not just on one's interests but on understanding those of all parties involved - to ensure both leave feeling content with the result while strengthening rather than weakening relations between them.

Negotiating parties should also consider future business opportunities and collaborations when engaging in negotiations. Even if their current negotiations don't result in desired results, it is still beneficial to keep an amicable relationship with both parties for potential future opportunities; maintaining such relations could open doors to further negotiations or collaborations in the future.

Thus, when approaching negotiations, it is key to keep long-term gains in mind and build and nurture relationships while still seeking short-term gains. By striking this balance between both factors negotiating parties can achieve mutually beneficial agreements while creating future collaborations and opportunities.

Effective and Clear Communication during Negotiations:

Effective negotiation communication is vital as it helps both sides understand each other's needs and goals. For successful negotiation sessions, clear, confident, and persuasive speech must be used throughout. One strategy to accomplish this goal is by setting forth an agenda at the outset that clearly details all topics to be covered during each negotiation session as well as any objectives to be reached.

Active listening is also key for effective negotiation communications. Focusing on and acknowledging another party's concerns will help build rapport and foster trust. In addition, active listening can give you insights into their priorities - information that could be used more persuasively when framing arguments.

Effective negotiation communication includes using language readily understood by both parties involved; instead of employing technical jargon or vague terms that might mislead your counterparts, use straightforward language to convey your points effectively.

Nonverbal communication plays an integral part in negotiations. Your body language, tone of voice, and facial expressions all convey more information than just what words do. Therefore, ensuring these nonverbal cues match your verbal message effectively is crucial. For example, maintaining eye contact, using appropriate gestures, and speaking confidently are all ways to convey your message effectively.

Effective communication is of utmost importance during negotiations, so it is imperative to practice and prepare ahead of time to ensure your message is understood by both parties involved.

Locating and Generating Mutually Beneficial Solutions: At any negotiation table, finding common ground can be key to reaching an amicable settlement. This involves identifying areas where both sides agree, then coming together to develop solutions that meet everyone's needs.

One effective strategy for finding common ground is identifying shared goals or interests. When they focus on what both parties hope to accomplish instead of their positions, negotiators can work collaboratively towards solutions that benefit all. For instance, an investor and a StartUp may share an interest in seeing each other succeed and expand - in which case, both could work toward creating an arrangement that helps the StartUp achieve growth while providing returns for both.

A good strategy for finding common ground is understanding each party's underlying needs. For instance, investors might demand more control in negotiations due to worries over a Startup's return on investment. By understanding this need and their concerns as part of negotiations, the StartUp can address both sets of requirements in acceptable ways to both sides.

Negotiators must also be open to compromise and look for win-win solutions, meaning being willing to give up something in exchange for something else in return. For instance, in negotiations regarding equity ownership, a StartUp might give up more ownership shares in exchange for receiving larger investments from an investor. By remaining flexible during these talks, negotiators can produce solutions that satisfy everyone's needs.

Finding common ground requires excellent communication skills, an openness to hearing the other party's perspective, and the commitment to work cooperatively toward finding mutually beneficial solutions. By emphasizing shared goals, recognizing underlying needs, and being willing to make concessions when necessary, negotiators can build trust while creating the foundation for long-term relationships.

Closing the Deal and Ensuring Follow-Through:

Closing a deal and ensuring follow-through are two essential components of successful negotiation, requiring close attention to detail and continuous follow-up. Once an agreement has been reached, it is vital that both parties understand all the terms of it as soon as possible and all paperwork related to it has been completed promptly, such as reviewing contracts, transferring funds, or fulfilling any other conditions of the agreement in a timely fashion.

To ensure a deal goes through smoothly, it's vital to establish clear lines of communication and maintain a professional demeanour. Both parties should be open and forthcoming about their intentions and expectations as soon as they arise, with any issues or concerns addressed immediately. Furthermore, being willing to make concessions when necessary can help build trust between both parties and form strong working relationships.

Once a deal has been finalized, all commitments made during negotiation must be honoured. This includes fulfilling any products or services promised as promised, paying any agreed-upon fees or royalties, and maintaining regular contact with one another to maintain strong and productive relationships.

Closing deals involves an intricate blend of planning, communication, and working collaboratively to find mutually beneficial results. By adhering to these key principles during negotiations, negotiators can increase their odds of success while building lasting and rewarding relationships with their counterparts.

Strategies for Building and Sustaining a Strong Negotiating Position:

Negotiations require a firm position to achieve your goals and secure the best deals possible. This requires thoroughly preparing, identifying your strengths and weaknesses, and understanding the priorities and interests of all parties involved. Here are some strategies:

1. **Thorough Preparation:** Before entering negotiations, it is crucial to gather all pertinent information and thoroughly understand the issues at stake. This may involve researching both parties' interests and negotiation styles, as well as your strengths and weaknesses.

2. **Establish Your Leverage Points**: Every negotiation includes issues or factors that are more significant to one party than another, which you can leverage for maximum effect in negotiations. Knowing and using these leverage points effectively can give your negotiations an edge and strengthen them.

3. **Have Multiple Options Available:** Any negotiation must have multiple options to increase flexibility and bargaining power. For example, developing multiple proposals or solutions and being open to adjusting your position as the negotiation progresses can give you more bargaining power and increase flexibility.

4. **Establish Credibility:** Trust can strengthen your negotiating position with the other party. Do this by being honest and open while showing expertise on the matter at hand.

5. **Keep Your Emotions Under Control:** Emotional reactions can erode your negotiating position, so it is vitally important that you remain calm and focused

during the negotiation process by managing your emotions and avoiding impulsive or reactive behaviours.

6. Maintain a Positive Relationship: While negotiations can be emotionally draining and trying, both parties must maintain positive relations during negotiations. This means communicating approachable and respectfully while actively listening to one another's perspectives in search of mutually beneficial solutions. Developing strong negotiating positions while building positive relationships increases the chances of securing favourable deals.

Exploit past negotiation experiences to strengthen and advance your negotiation abilities:

Learning from past negotiation experiences and continually honing your negotiation skills are essential to any business owner or entrepreneur's strategy. Negotiation is an art that takes practice to master, so the more often you engage in negotiations, the better you'll become at them.

One effective way of learning from past experiences is to debrief after every negotiation, reflecting on what went well and what didn't. Pose questions such as, "What did I do right in that negotiation?" and "How could I have improved its outcome?" Then, consider your goals before starting the negotiation, and evaluate whether you achieved them.

Another effective strategy for honing your negotiation skills is seeking feedback from others who have negotiated similar deals. Gather their insights on what worked well and what didn't, then use those learnings to shape your approach to negotiation. Attend negotiation workshops or courses online that teach new techniques you can implement during negotiations.

Apart from learning from past experiences, it's also crucial to refine and perfect your negotiation skills on an ongoing basis. Read books and articles on negotiation techniques; practice in low-stakes situations; seek negotiation opportunities whenever they present themselves; the more you practice, the more confident and effective you will become and increase the odds of funding your business venture.

Negotiating funding deals effectively is essential for any entrepreneur wishing to expand their business. Mastering the basics, different negotiation styles, and prioritizing points are crucial elements to master. In addition, approach negotiations with an understanding of your goals and expectations and research about and research of your counterpart; building rapport and trust are also integral to successful negotiations, and effective communication is key to a successful negotiation outcome.

Maintaining emotional control, setting your BATNA, finding common ground, and creating mutually beneficial solutions are among the many key techniques for successful negotiations. Furthermore, closing deals quickly, ensuring follow-through, and developing and maintaining strong negotiating positions are integral elements of ensuring their success.

Negotiation is an art that can be learned and refined over time, so draw upon past negotiation experiences to continue honing and perfecting your negotiation abilities for future endeavours. By keeping these essential tips and strategies in mind, you'll approach any negotiation confidently and increase the odds of securing your Startup's funding for success.

Chapter 28
Pitching to Corporate Investors

Strategies for Success

Corporate investors can be a valuable source of funding for StartUps looking to grow and scale their businesses. Unlike angel or venture capitalist investors, corporate investors are established companies who make strategic investments to further the goals of other organizations - whether that is acquiring new technology, expanding into new markets, or diversifying product offerings.

Pitching to corporate investors requires a different approach than pitching to other investors. As corporate investors may seek both strategic partnership or acquisition opportunities and financial returns on their investments, StartUps should tailor their pitch specifically for the goals and interests of each corporate investor they are targeting.

This chapter focuses on strategies and best practices for pitching successfully to corporate investors. From identifying prospective corporate investors to developing pitches that resonate with their strategic goals, this chapter offers valuable insight and actionable tips that can help StartUp founders or aspiring entrepreneurs secure funding from corporate investors.

Understanding Corporate and Traditional Investors:

Knowing the difference between corporate and traditional investors is crucial when seeking funding for your StartUp. While traditional investors such as angel investors or venture capitalists provide equity investments to StartUps in exchange for equity stakes, corporate investors are usually established companies who invest either as strategic partners or for financial gain in new businesses.

Corporate investors offer StartUps more than financial support; they may bring invaluable networks, expertise, and resources that help StartUps expand and scale more quickly. However, it is important to remember that corporate investors may have different goals and expectations when investing than traditional investors.

One key difference between corporate and traditional investors lies in their investment focus. Traditional investors prioritize financial returns, while corporate investors may also seek access to technologies, products, or markets through investments. Therefore, when pitching to corporate investors, StartUps must demonstrate how their products or services align with strategic goals and their financial potential when pitching them.

Another key distinction lies in the relationship between investors and StartUps. While traditional investors tend to take a more passive role, corporate investors may take an active role in their operations and strategy - potentially leading to conflicts if goals or priorities differ significantly. Therefore, it is crucial for StartUps to carefully review any investment agreement with corporate investors to maintain independence and control of their operations.

Understanding the differences between corporate and traditional investors is vital when developing an approach for pitching to corporate investors. Tailoring your presentation to their needs and priorities and carefully considering any investment agreement can increase the Startup's odds of securing funding and creating successful partnerships with corporate investors.

Determining the Pros and Cons of Pitching to Corporate Investors:

Understanding the advantages and disadvantages of pitching to corporate investors is an integral step for StartUps looking for funding. Corporate investors differ significantly from traditional investors in many ways; taking note of these distinctions will enable StartUps to determine whether pursuing corporate funding is the ideal path.

One advantage of pitching to corporate investors can be accessing their wide array of resources. Not only can corporate investors offer financial backing, but they often also have access to knowledge, networks, and distribution channels that may prove invaluable for StartUps. Furthermore, corporate investors might be interested in strategic partnerships that give access to new customers while providing market intelligence.

There can be drawbacks to pitching to corporate investors, however. A potential issue could be losing control of your Startup's vision and direction to external forces like corporate investors, who may have different agendas that conflict with your goals. Furthermore, pitching to corporate investors requires extensive due diligence, which could delay investment decisions and prove challenging when StartUps require quick answers quickly.

Before approaching corporate investors for investment,

StartUps should carefully weigh their benefits and drawbacks. This way, potential risks must be balanced against potential gains while ensuring their goals and values match the investors. As a result, StartUps increase their chances of success when pitching them.

Potential Corporate Investors and their Investment Goals:

Researching corporate investors and understanding their investment goals are integral to pitching to them successfully. Unlike traditional investors, corporate investors possess specific criteria when evaluating investments that often reflect strategic goals for the corporation and industry/sector conditions in which it operates.

As part of your research into potential corporate investors, it is crucial that you first gain a thorough understanding of the industry landscape and identify companies that align strategically with your business. Then, once identified as potential corporate investors, it is necessary to research their investment goals and objectives; this may involve reviewing annual reports, press releases, and other forms of public information and attending industry conferences or networking events.

When considering potential corporate investors, assessing their advantages and disadvantages when pitching to them is essential. Investors typically bring abundant resources such as distribution channels, technology solutions, industry knowledge, and ongoing support that could aid your company's expansion.

Pitching to corporate investors comes with its own set of risks. You should carefully assess these potential drawbacks to determine if pitching to corporate investors is right for your business. Such issues could include concerns over loss of control over your business and conflicts of interest that could occur between investors. You must carefully evaluate these factors to ascertain if this approach to funding your business will provide long-term growth.

Customize your Pitch to Meet the Interests and Goals of Corporate Investors:

Tailoring your pitch to meet corporate investors' specific interests and goals is key to successfully securing funding from them. Corporate investors typically have specific investment criteria and goals they're striving towards, which they look for StartUps that can help achieve. So you must research and gain an understanding of any corporate investors you plan on pitching your idea.

Study their previous investments and search for trends or themes. This will indicate which types of StartUps they might prefer investing in while you can also review their website, annual reports, and press releases to gain a fuller picture of their overall strategy and goals. Once you understand a corporate investor's interests and goals, it becomes easier to craft your pitch so it speaks directly to those interests. This may involve emphasizing aspects of your StartUp that align with their investment criteria or showing how you can help them meet strategic goals through partnership.

Corporate investors tend to have different priorities than traditional investors. For example, they might prioritize acquiring technology or intellectual property to integrate into existing products or services. At the same time, StartUps might provide access to new markets or increase customer base expansion.

By tailoring your pitch to meet corporate investors' unique interests and goals, you can increase your chances of securing funding and creating long-term relationships with them.

Breaking Down Barriers with Corporate Investors Before and After Pitch:

Building relationships with corporate investors is integral to successfully pitching to them. Before initiating any pitch discussions with them, you should establish rapport by networking and attending events where potential investors are likely to participate - this gives you a chance to introduce yourself and gain more information on their investment goals and strategies.

As another way of developing relationships with corporate investors, researching them and their companies can help. Doing this will enable you to better understand their priorities, values, and investment history - providing valuable information on which to tailor your approach and show them you understand their interests.

At your pitch, be sure to show enthusiasm and passion for your StartUp while communicating how its goals align with those of investors. Be open to feedback or questions from the investor, as this provides a chance for further relationship-building with them.

After your pitch, follow up with investors and thank them for participating. Provide updates about progress and milestones while maintaining relationships; this could open the door for future investment opportunities and partnerships.

Establishing relationships with corporate investors takes time and effort but can greatly increase your chances of funding and support for your StartUp. Communicating the unique value proposition of your StartUp to corporate investors:

Communicating the unique value proposition of your StartUp to potential corporate investors is vital when pitching it for funding. Ensure your potential investor understands what sets you apart in your industry and how your product or service solves its unique problems innovatively. Outline clearly who your target market is and clearly state the problem(s) being solved using your product/service as starting points for this conversation.

Communicating your value proposition to corporate investors requires emphasizing its benefits to their organization - increased revenue, improved efficiency, or a superior customer experience. Remember to tailor your presentation to their needs and goals when pitching to individual corporate investors.

Communicating your value proposition includes showing its scalability. Corporate investors often look for companies with significant growth potential that provide an attractive return on their investments; using market size, revenue projections, and growth strategies as evidence of such potential can make your pitch even more convincing.

Ensure your value proposition is communicated using clear and direct language when discussing its benefits to corporate investors. Avoid technical jargon that might confuse them; focus on communicating your message clearly while emphasizing your Startup's key advantages and unique aspects.

Highlight the Potential Synergies and Advantages of Working with Corporate Investors:

Emphasizing the potential synergies and benefits of partnering with corporate investors is integral to pitching them successfully. StartUps must show how their product or service aligns with their business strategy, providing value through a partnership with your StartUp. It would help if you highlighted any synergies or benefits your partnership with them may bring as part of their pitch.

Before pitching to corporate investors, you must gain an in-depth knowledge of their business model and strategy. This will enable you to tailor your pitch and emphasize how your

StartUp can enhance existing operations, highlight its unique value proposition, offer competitive advantages, and help corporate investor meet their goals.

As part of your partnership with your StartUp, consider the long-term benefits. For example, discuss how your StartUp could give corporate investors an edge, reduce costs or create new revenue streams while emphasizing how a partnership could result in new products or services being developed, expanded markets, or accessing customers that weren't there before.

By emphasizing the potential synergies and benefits of partnering with your StartUp, you can convince corporate investors to invest in it as a smart business move. Furthermore, trust and credibility can be built between the parties involved by showing that you know their business well enough and how your StartUp can assist them in meeting their goals more easily.

Preparing for Due Diligence with Corporate Investors:

Planning for their due diligence process is crucial when approaching corporate investors for funding. Due diligence refers to how investors evaluate any prospective investment - it entails evaluating the viability and potential risks as part of an evaluation process that is time-consuming yet integral in getting investment commitment from corporate investors.

As part of due diligence preparations, StartUps should have a comprehensive grasp on their finances - revenue, costs, cash flow projections, and an outline of their product or service offering. A strong team with the necessary skills should also be in place.

StartUps should also be prepared to answer questions regarding their intellectual property, such as patents, trademarks, and copyrights. In addition, corporate investors are likely to inquire into potential risks and returns associated with this area; therefore, StartUps must gain in-depth knowledge about this aspect.

StartUps should also be prepared to present documentation related to regulatory compliance, such as licenses and permits. This can be essential when seeking investors, especially for industries with strict regulations.

Finalize the due diligence process by being open with corporate investors during due diligence. Be honest about any risks or challenges, and be ready to address any concerns. By showing their willingness to work with corporate investors, StartUps may increase their odds of securing funding from these sources.

Negotiating and Closing Deals with Corporate Investors:

After successfully pitching to corporate investors and passing due diligence processes, the next step should be negotiating and finalizing the deal. Negotiations are often complex and challenging as both sides seek to protect their interests - it is key that both parties come into this negotiation stage with clear expectations about what you want to accomplish with this partnership. It is also a key point to remember that negotiations be approached strategically to achieve optimal outcomes and value for your StartUp company.

Considerations should also be given to how corporate investors could affect your Startup's culture and autonomy when negotiating. You need to negotiate terms that protect your vision while giving you control over key decisions; at the same time, corporate investors may have specific expectations of the partnership; it is also a key point that both parties come to an agreement that suits both.

Another aspect to remember when structuring any deal is its structure, including funding type and amount, as well as any equity or ownership stakes. One must understand the ramifications of various financing and ownership structures, such as debt financing, preferred stock, or common stock ownership stakes and structures, for optimal funding with fair and reasonable ownership structures. A skilled negotiator can assist in finding terms that provide sufficient funding while upholding equitable ownership structures.

Negotiations with corporate investors often encompass more than financial terms alone; negotiations may include aspects such as intellectual property rights, resource access, or strategic support beyond simple money transactions. When considering these non-financial aspects of a partnership agreement, it's crucial to negotiate terms that meet your Startup's goals.

Once negotiations are complete, the final step in concluding a deal should be sealing it by signing agreements and transferring funds. All legal and regulatory requirements must be fulfilled while both parties understand their responsibilities and obligations regarding closing the deal.

Negotiating and closing deals with corporate investors requires careful preparation, effective communication, and in-depth knowledge of your Startup's value. By taking an appropriate approach, you can secure partnerships that help your StartUp expand and thrive while upholding your vision and autonomy.

Manage Post-Investment Relations with Corporate Investors:

Maintaining positive relations with corporate investors after closing the deal and receiving funding is as essential to its success as closing itself. Therefore, regular communication, transparency, and the willingness to collaborate toward mutual success are vitally important when building long-term relationships between business partners.

One of the first steps in successfully managing post-investment relationships is establishing open lines of communication with your corporate investor. This means scheduling regular meetings or calls to keep them informed on your progress, discussing any challenges or concerns that arise, and obtaining their advice or guidance as necessary. It's essential to remain transparent and honest when communicating with each other, even when things don't go quite according to plan.

Meeting their expectations is an integral aspect of managing the relationship with corporate investors. This means fulfilling your promises during your pitch or due diligence process and communicating any changes or developments that could alter their investment plans. Furthermore, be open and accepting of feedback or suggestions from them, as they could provide invaluable resources that help grow and scale your business.

As well as regularly communicating and meeting expectations, fostering a close working relationship with your corporate investor is essential. This means promoting trust and collaboration while showing your commitment to the partnership through responsiveness to their needs and requests while going the extra mile in providing value and results.

Managing post-investment relationships with corporate investors requires an active and collaborative approach. By staying open with communication, meeting expectations, and creating strong rapport between the parties involved, you can ensure your partnership will be mutually beneficial and successful.

Pitching to corporate investors can be a viable funding solution for StartUps looking to expand and scale their businesses. However, approaching corporate investors requires a slightly different approach than pitching traditional investors since they are looking for potential strategic partnerships and synergies within their portfolio companies. Therefore, StartUps must conduct extensive research before approaching these corporate investors by conducting the appropriate due diligence on them in terms of goals and values alignment and tailoring their pitch accordingly.

Establishing and cultivating relationships with corporate investors are essential to securing funding and creating effective partnerships. StartUps must prepare to undergo an intensive due diligence process before entering negotiations and closing deals that benefit both parties. Furthermore, managing post-investment relationships between corporate investors is imperative for long-term success and requires clear communication and ongoing collaboration.

By following these strategies and tips, StartUps can increase their chances of pitching corporate investors successfully and securing funding to reach their growth and scalability objectives.

◆◆◆

Chapter 29
Funding Options beyond Equity for StartUps

It's Advisable to Weigh Other Options

When StartUps seek funding, equity financing through angel investors or venture capitalists is often their go-to solution. But other financing solutions better meet certain businesses' needs: alternative options can offer financing without giving up ownership and control, making this approach suitable for StartUps that have yet to see revenue generation or profitability.

In this chapter, we will discuss alternative financing options available to StartUps and how best to pitch them effectively. We will discuss their advantages, disadvantages, appropriateness for various business types, and tips on preparing an effective pitch. By understanding these alternatives to equity financing and developing effective pitch techniques for them, StartUps may increase their chances of securing sufficient funding.

Understanding alternative financing options available to StartUps:

Apart from equity financing, StartUps have many alternative financing options to raise funds for their businesses. Being aware of all available alternative financing solutions is important as each funding option possesses different characteristics, benefits, and drawbacks; some popular alternatives for StartUps include:

1. **Debt Financing:** Debt financing is an attractive financing solution for StartUps that involves borrowing money from banks, investors or financial institutions with the agreement to repay it back over a set period with interest payments. The most popular and common forms of debt financing for StartUps include bank loans, lines of credit, and credit cards. Loans may be against a collateral security or without one, but an interest element is always there.

2. **Crowd funding**: Crowd funding refers to raising funds from multiple individuals via online platforms, often in a donation, rewards, or equity-based model. Various kinds of crowd funding exist, including donation-based, rewards-based, and equity-based.

3. **Revenue Based Financing:** Revenue-based financing is an alternative funding source where investors provide funds in exchange for a percentage of future revenues from a Startup's revenue stream. It can be particularly effective for StartUps that can forecast their revenues accurately.

4. **Asset Based Financing:** Asset-based financing involves taking out a loan secured against assets owned by your business, such as equipment, inventory, or accounts receivable.

Government Grants:

Grants are non-repayable funds governments, foundations, or other organizations provide to fund specific projects or initiatives. It's essential for StartUps to carefully evaluate each financing option available and select one that meets their business needs and goals.

Advantages and Disadvantages of Alternative Financing Solutions versus Equity Financing:

Alternative financing options provide an attractive and flexible method for funding your StartUp business. They have several advantages over traditional equity financing; equity requires giving up equity in your company to investors; alternative financing options, on the other hand, do not necessitate this sacrifice and allow you to retain full control and decision-making power over your enterprise.

Alternative financing solutions are quicker and simpler to secure than equity financing since they don't involve as much due diligence or legal processes. Furthermore, alternative loans offer greater flexibility with repayment terms and interest rates, such as revenue-based financing, which allows repayment based on a percentage of your revenue rather than fixed monthly payments.

Alternative financing options do come with some drawbacks. For example, they tend to be more costly than traditional bank loans or equity financing due to higher interest rates and fees; moreover, some alternative funding solutions require personal guarantees or collateral that could put your assets at risk should your business default on repayment its loans.

Before pursuing alternative financing solutions, it is vital that you carefully weigh their advantages and disadvantages to determine which option best meets your business needs and goals. Here's how you can make this determination:

Equity financing though preferable, may not always be the right solution for StartUps, and alternative funding can offer benefits like increased control of your company, less ownership dilution, and increased repayment flexibility. But these financing alternatives come with risks that StartUps must carefully evaluate before considering them as viable financing solutions.

One important consideration when seeking alternative financing options for StartUps is the stage at which it operates. For example, revenue-based financing or factoring may be best suited for established revenue streams; however, StartUps still in the early stages of development may only have access to equity financing as an alternative financing source. Furthermore, your industry of operation could influence how suitable alternative financing solutions may be; those operating in industries with predictable cash flows might find revenue-based financing more suitable; those involved with long product development cycles may struggle more to obtain short-term loans.

Another key consideration for StartUps requiring significant financing is the amount and timing. While alternative financing may have lower funding caps than traditional equity funding, StartUps that require significant amounts may need to explore multiple financing solutions to meet their funding requirements. Factoring may be particularly effective at meeting short-term cash flow needs while crowd funding offers longer funding cycles and other advantages like increased customer engagement.

StartUps should carefully weigh the trade-offs between equity financing and alternative funding options before selecting one to finance their company. For example, while alternative financing may provide greater control of their company with a reduced dilution of ownership, such as alternative lending may come with higher interest rates, shorter repayment terms, or more restrictive covenants than equity funding - StartUps must carefully evaluate these factors in light of their long-term financial goals to choose an ideal financing solution for them.

StartUps must carefully consider their stage of development, industry, funding needs, and long-term financial goals when making informed decisions regarding alternative financing options for their business. By carefully weighing up each financing option and their advantages and disadvantages against one another and their circumstances, StartUps can make more informed choices regarding how best to finance their growth while reaching their business objectives.

Formulate a Comprehensive Financing Strategy Combining Equity and Alternative Forms of Funding:

When financing a StartUp, various options exist beyond traditional equity funding. Debt financing, grants, and crowd funding offer StartUps access to capital without giving away equity - though each option has pros and cons.

One approach for taking advantage of both equity and alternative financing strategies is creating an all-encompassing financing plan that uses both methods simultaneously. By diversifying capital sources while mitigating risk, StartUps can reduce risks while diversifying funding sources.

The first step in developing an effective financing strategy for StartUps is identifying their funding needs. This includes determining how much capital is necessary and its intended use. Once identified, StartUps can begin exploring various financing options that may suit them.

Equity financing can be an ideal solution for StartUps seeking large amounts of capital in exchange for giving up equity. But StartUps that do not yet feel ready or require smaller amounts may consider alternative funding methods like debt or grant funding.

Debt financing options such as loans or lines of credit may be appropriate for StartUps with steady sources of revenue and the capacity to make regular payments. Grants are another popular source of funding, especially among tech or social impact StartUps that don't require repayment of any funds received.

Crowd funding has quickly become a more popular alternative financing solution in recent years, allowing StartUps to raise smaller amounts from numerous individuals through online platforms. Crowd funding may serve as a good way to generate excitement about an idea while validating it - though it might not provide sufficient capital on an ongoing basis.

At its core, creating an effective financing strategy involves finding your Startup's optimal mix of funding options. By diversifying sources of capital and mitigating risk, your venture can set itself up for long-term success.

Pitching Lenders for Debt Financing: While equity financing may be the go-to form of StartUp funding, debt financing can also be an option worth exploring for many StartUps. Debt financing entails borrowing money from lenders at interest over an agreed-upon timeframe. Banks, credit unions, and online lenders may all provide this form of capital.

To be successful at pitching lenders for debt financing, StartUps must demonstrate an in-depth knowledge of their financial needs and articulate how the borrowed funds will be used to produce an ROI. A solid business plan is also key, including financial projections and proof that debt has been responsibly managed.

StartUps seeking loan funding should also be prepared to

discuss their credit history and any collateral they might offer as security for a loan. Lenders will look for evidence of steady cash flows; personal guarantees from founders or other stakeholders may be necessary for this loan application.

StartUps may also consider alternative lenders like online lending platforms as potential financing partners for their venture. Such platforms typically provide faster and more flexible lending solutions than banks and credit unions, although their interest rates and repayment terms may be more stringent than conventional institutions.

Debt financing requires a special business case with strong financial credentials and an informative presentation tailored specifically toward meeting lender concerns and requirements.

Tips for Crafting an Engaging Campaign and Connecting with Investors on Crowd Funding Platforms:

Crowd funding has quickly become one of the go-to financing methods for StartUps. Crowd funding platforms provide entrepreneurs with an avenue for pitching their idea to a wide pool of potential investors and raising funds through small contributions from numerous individuals. However, to run an effective crowd funding campaign, entrepreneurs must craft an eye-catching pitch that attracts investors' interest.

Having a clear and concise message is one key to running a successful crowd funding campaign. Entrepreneurs must articulate effectively the problem their StartUp is trying to solve and why their solution is unique and innovative. Furthermore, it is vitally important that they set clear and specific goals for the campaign and communicate them to potential investors.

An integral component of a successful crowd funding campaign is an eye-catching and user-friendly page. A good campaign page should provide easy navigation, full information about the Startup's products or services, and high-quality images and videos showcasing its value proposition.

Entrepreneurs should also offer rewards or incentives as part of their crowd funding campaign, whether that means early access to products or services or exclusive merchandise or experiences. Offering rewards will incentivize investors and increase the chance that they contribute.

Entrepreneurs must engage with potential investors and supporters throughout their crowd funding campaign. This may involve providing regular updates about its progress and StartUp development and responding to backers' questions and comments. Forming an engaged community around their campaign can generate buzz that attracts additional investment capital.

Pitching crowd funding platforms requires a well-planned and executed campaign that effectively communicates a Startup's value proposition while creating buzz among potential investors. By following these tips and best practices, entrepreneurs can increase their odds of implementing a successful crowd funding campaign and securing alternative financing for their StartUp.

Pitching to Venture Debt Providers: Key Considerations and Best Practices for Negotiation Terms:

Pitching venture debt providers involves seeking non-dilutive financing solutions to assist StartUps without further diluting equity. Most lenders specialize in providing non-dilutive venture debt for early-stage StartUps and growth-stage businesses with strong revenue streams but may not yet be profitable.

To secure venture debt, StartUps need to demonstrate they

can consistently generate consistent revenues, create a sound business plan, and possess a realistic roadmap towards profitability. Furthermore, StartUps should display strong market knowledge as well as possess an achievable growth plan.

StartUps should research potential venture debt providers and familiarize themselves with their specific lending criteria and preferences to tailor their pitch and increase the chance of receiving financing.

StartUps looking for venture debt should come prepared to negotiate key terms when pitching venture debt providers, including interest rates, repayment schedules, and covenants. Furthermore, StartUps should review all loan agreements carefully to make sure that they fully understand all terms and conditions pertaining to them.

Pitching to venture debt providers can be a valuable option for StartUps seeking to expand their operations without incurring significant dilution. However, success requires a firm grasp of the lending process and an approach to conveying the Startup's value to prospective lenders.

Strategies for Pitching Revenue-Based Financing Options:

Revenue-based financing (RBF) is an innovative alternative financing method that enables StartUps to raise funds against future revenue instead of loans or equity financing, unlike conventional forms, which may require founders to give up equity or make regular fixed payments; instead, investors receive a percentage of your Startup's future earnings until an investor has repaid an agreed-upon sum.

When pitching to RBF providers, it's key to emphasize the predictability and stability of your revenue stream. RBF investors prefer companies with a track record of consistently generating consistent revenues over an extended period. Providing financial projections or historical performance data may prove beneficial.

An important element in pitching RBF investments is negotiating the terms of the agreement. StartUps should be ready to negotiate the percentage of revenue to be shared with investors and the repayment period length to find an ideal balance between how much funding can be raised and any adverse effect this revenue share might have on company finances.

StartUps must also consider the possible drawbacks of Revenue Based Financing (RBF). For example, if they experience prolonged revenue decline and their investor ends up with more of the company's earnings than anticipated, this may limit their ability to reinvest or pursue other forms of funding.

To reduce these risks, it's crucial that companies carefully review any RBF agreement and whether its terms align with their long-term business goals. Then, with an understanding of its advantages and disadvantages and a pitch showcasing its revenue stream strengths, StartUps may successfully secure this alternative form of financing.

Government Grants and Subsidies in Alternative Financing:

Government grants and subsidies are an increasingly vital source of alternative financing for StartUps. Governments worldwide often provide grants and subsidies for businesses aligned with their priorities - such as innovative technologies or those working on social and environmental issues - making these a key source of alternative finance for newcomers. Such support comes in various forms, such as research grants, business development grants, tax credits, or subsidies for specific industries.

Securing government grants and subsidies can be an involved and time-consuming process, often requiring extensive research to identify relevant grant programs and subsidies, crafting an interesting business case to align with their goals, and submitting a comprehensive grant application demonstrating its impact. StartUps must also meet eligibility criteria such as company size, location, nature of project, etc.

Government grants and subsidies can offer significant advantages to StartUps beyond financial support. Achieve validation from receiving government support increases your reputation and credibility while opening doors for further investment and partnerships. Furthermore, government resources and expertise help speed up their growth to help achieve goals more quickly.

As an alternative source of financing, StartUps pursuing government grants and subsidies should carefully assess both the potential advantages and drawbacks of such programs and their eligibility criteria and specific requirements. In addition, they must align with the long-term strategic goals of the business without placing undue restrictions on operations or growth.

Establish a Multifaceted Financing Strategy Comprising Equity and Alternative Sources:

Establishing a robust financing plan for any StartUp looking to raise funds is essential to success. By including various equity and alternative funding options, StartUps can reduce risk while improving the chances of receiving necessary funds. The first step towards creating such a diversified financing strategy should be assessing all of their financing needs as well as available options.

Despite being the most preferred funding option, equity financing comes with certain drawbacks, such as ownership dilution and loss of control. Other financing solutions, including debt financing, crowd funding, revenue-based financing, or government grants and subsidies, can offer funding without these pitfalls.

Once financing options have been evaluated, StartUps should create a financing strategy incorporating equity and alternative forms of funding, considering their current financial standing, growth potential, and risk tolerance.

Step two in successfully pitching your StartUp to potential investors is crafting an engaging pitch highlighting its unique selling points, growth potential, and financial projections. Furthermore, it should detail how funds will be utilized as well as how investors will reap returns from their investments.

StartUps must regularly assess and revise their financing strategy as the business develops. This may require raising additional capital or refinancing debt, exploring new financing avenues, or raising additional debt. By having a comprehensive financing strategy in place, StartUps can better manage finances, reduce risks, and increase their chances of success.

Legal and Regulatory Considerations for Alternative Financing Options:

As with any financing solution, alternative financing options come with their own set of legal and regulatory considerations that StartUps must be mindful of when selecting any alternative funding source. Therefore, it is vitally important that StartUps understand these implications before selecting any alternative funding source.

Some alternative financing options, such as crowd funding and revenue-based financing, must comply with specific regulations and requirements, such as filing disclosure documents, adhering to marketing guidelines, and complying with investor protection laws. Failing to comply may result in fines or legal action being taken.

StartUps considering revenue-based financing must also understand its legal and contractual ramifications, including any favourable repayment schedule, interest rates, or restrictions on how the funds may be spent.

StartUps wishing to apply for government grants and subsidies should know the eligibility criteria and application processes. In addition, many grants and subsidies require StartUps to meet certain deadlines, with additional financial information necessary for processing.

StartUps seeking alternative financing should seek guidance from legal and financial professionals with experience in these areas to navigate the legal and regulatory pitfalls associated with their chosen financing options and ensure successful financing strategies. By adhering to relevant regulations, StartUps can avoid potential legal or financial pitfalls and ensure a successful financing strategy.

Management of Repayment Processes for Debt Financing and Meeting Grant Funding Criteria:

Repaying debt financing or revenue-based financing, and fulfilling grant funding requirements, can be challenging but essential in maintaining positive relations with investors and meeting legal obligations. When it comes to debt financing, having an in-depth knowledge of your repayment schedule and having enough funds available when payments are due is paramount; otherwise, penalties and credit damage could make securing financing more challenging.

Revenue-based financing requires closely tracking revenue streams to ensure that an agreed-upon percentage of revenue is going toward repayment, as well as communicating regularly with your revenue-based investors and keeping them updated on your business performance.

It is crucial that when applying for government grants and subsidies, one understands the terms and requirements for each program. This could involve providing regular reports on your business performance or using funds for specific purposes; failure to adhere could result in losing funding altogether or legal action being taken against your company.

As always, it is vital to maintain open channels of communication with investors and funding providers. Sharing regular updates about your business performance and any modifications to repayment schedules can build trust between the parties involved and ensure everyone stays on the same page. Also, seek professional guidance from lawyers or accountants to make sure you comply with all legal and regulatory requirements.

StartUps have many financing options beyond traditional equity financing to choose from. By understanding each type of financing option and its pros and cons for your StartUp, as well as which fits best, a comprehensive financing strategy that incorporates both equity and alternative funding can be devised that combines these funding sources for greater capital diversification, risk mitigation, and financial flexibility.

Pitching to lenders, crowd funding platforms, venture debt providers, and revenue-based financing options requires specific strategies and techniques to communicate your Startup's value proposition and secure financing effectively. It's also crucial that StartUps understand what these alternative financing providers look for when evaluating StartUps, such as revenue growth, market size, and management team experience. These all come into play during the evaluation processes.

Maintaining repayment processes and meeting grant funding requirements require careful legal and regulatory attention. A strong understanding of your financing agreement terms and working closely with the legal team is vital to ensure compliance.

By carefully considering their financing options and understanding their requirements and opportunities, StartUps can secure the necessary capital.

Chapter 30
Navigating Legal Considerations

How to Ensure Compliance and Mitigate Risks

It is a challenging and exciting journey to start a business. You will have to make many important decisions along the way. Navigating the legal landscape is an important part of building a StartUp, as it involves complying with laws and regulations while minimizing risks. Therefore, it is important to know the legal implications of your business, whether you are launching a new venture or expanding a current one.

This chapter will examine the most important legal issues for entrepreneurs and StartUps, such as protecting intellectual property, privacy, contract negotiation, and employment laws. This chapter will give you practical advice on overcoming these challenges, ensuring compliance with applicable laws and regulations, and mitigating risks for your business. Understanding and addressing legal considerations will help you build a solid foundation for your company and achieve your goals.

Understanding the Legal Landscape of StartUps:

StartUps are constantly operating in an ever-changing legal environment. Entrepreneurs need to be aware of the legal requirements and considerations that are part and parcel of starting and operating a business. Complying with all central, state, and local laws and regulations is important.

The first step in navigating your legal landscape as a StartUp is to choose the right legal structure. You may form a corporation, LLC, or limited liability company. Each legal structure comes with its own set of advantages and disadvantages, as well as specific legal requirements.

Also, intellectual property, contracts, labour laws, data security and privacy, and tax compliance are important considerations. Understanding legal requirements and best practices will help entrepreneurs reduce legal risks and ensure compliance.

It can be difficult to navigate the legal landscape as a StartUp, but this is crucial for long-term success. Staying up to date on the latest legal requirements, and seeking advice from legal professionals with experience, allows entrepreneurs to ensure compliance, minimize legal risks, and focus on their business.

How to Incorporate Your Business and Choose the Best Legal Structure:

The legal structure of your new company is one of the key decisions that you must make when starting a business. This decision will affect everything, from taxation to personal liability, in case of a legal problem. StartUps are most commonly organized as a sole proprietary concern, a partnership, a limited liability partnership (LLP), or a company.

The sole proprietorship is a straightforward legal structure. One person is the sole proprietor and is responsible for the entire business. A partnership is similar to a sole proprietorship, but it involves more than one owner who shares the profits and responsibilities of the business.

A flexible LLP structure offers its owners limited liability protection, which means promoters cannot be held responsible in their capacity for the debts and liabilities of the company.

A corporation is an independent legal entity that provides the best protection against personal liability. This is a complicated legal structure that has strict reporting and governance requirements. However, it can provide certain tax advantages and make funding easier.

The right legal structure is important for your StartUp. You should carefully consider your goals, priorities, and other factors, such as your need for liability protection and tax implications. A legal professional can guide you through this process.

Intellectual Property Protection and Management:

Intellectual property is a crucial aspect of any StartUp. It provides a competitive edge and protects the innovative products and services of the company. Therefore, StartUps must understand intellectual property such as trademarks, patents, copyrights, and trade secrets and their legal protection.

Patents are granted to inventors by the government and give them exclusive rights that prevent anyone else from manufacturing, using, selling, or importing their inventions for a specific period. Companies use trademarks to protect their brand, which includes their logo, name, and other identifying marks. Copyrights protect creative works such as music, books, software, and art. Trade secrets are confidential business information such as customer lists and manufacturing processes. They provide a competitive edge and must not be disclosed.

StartUps should perform a comprehensive IP Audit to identify their valuable assets and protect them. This process includes assessing the Startup's current and future IP requirements, identifying key assets that need to be protected, creating strategies for protecting these assets, and implementing the strategy.

StartUps should also be aware that infringement of intellectual property rights can have serious consequences. Infringement suits can be expensive and damage a Startup's image. Therefore, you must do your due diligence to ensure you don't violate anyone else's intellectual property.

Contract Law and Negotiation Strategies:

StartUps need to understand contract law and negotiate strategies as they work with customers, vendors, investors, and other stakeholders. Understanding the basics of negotiation and contract law can help StartUps to avoid legal disputes and ensure all parties are clear on the terms of any agreement.

StartUps need to understand the various types of contracts in contract law. These include employment agreements, confidentiality agreements, and service contracts. Also, they need to know the basic elements of a contractual agreement, such as offer, acceptance, and consideration. Contract law covers other issues, such as termination, dispute resolution, and breach of contract.

StartUps need effective negotiation strategies when

negotiating with investors, partners, suppliers, and others. StartUps must understand their negotiation position, set realistic objectives, and communicate effectively with the other side. Finding areas of agreement and discord and finding ways to compromise are essential. StartUps should also be ready to walk away if terms aren't favourable or they don't feel the other party is negotiating in good faith.

Compliance with Industry-Specific Regulations:

StartUps must comply with regulations specific to their industry. This ensures they are operating within the law and avoiding potential legal risks. As a result, StartUps may be subjected to different regulations depending on their industry. These regulations include health and safety, environmental, data protection, and financial regulations.

StartUps should be aware of all the rules and regulations applicable to their sector, so they can take the necessary steps to ensure compliance. This could include obtaining licenses, and permits, adhering to specific standards, and implementing monitoring and compliance processes.

If you fail to adhere to industry-specific regulations, there may be legal consequences, such as fines and penalties. You could even face legal action. This can damage a Startup's reputation and make it more difficult to attract investors.

StartUps must work with experts in the field who can help them comply with relevant regulations. By ensuring compliance with regulations, StartUps can reduce legal risks and create a solid foundation for success.

How to Manage Legal Risks and Crises:

Legal risks and crises will always be present in a new business. These risks are costly, both in time and money. It is, therefore, important to manage legal risks proactively and be prepared for any potential crisis.

Establishing legal protocols and procedures is a great way to reduce legal risk. Create internal policies on data privacy, employee contracts, and intellectual property. Also, ensure that you comply with industry-specific regulations. To ensure that these protocols remain effective and relevant, reviewing and updating them regularly is important.

StartUps should have a plan for handling legal crises in addition to protocols and procedures. Having a crisis team, identifying potential legal issues, and creating an action plan are important.

StartUps should put communication and transparency first when a legal crisis occurs. It is important to inform stakeholders and customers of the situation and be transparent about the steps to resolve the issue.

StartUps can protect their reputation, financial health, and reputation by proactively managing legal risks.

Raising Capital while Maintaining Compliance with Securities Laws:

Raising capital to grow a StartUp is essential, but you must do it in accordance with securities laws. These laws were designed to protect investors against fraud and ensure that securities are traded honestly and transparently. If you fail to follow securities laws, there can be severe consequences, including fines and court action. Therefore, StartUps must be familiar with securities laws and work closely with legal counsel to ensure compliance.

The difference between private and public offerings is an important factor to consider. Private offerings are restricted to a small group of investors, whereas public offerings include the sale of securities to a general audience. StartUps usually conduct private offerings that are subject to exemptions from securities laws. Regulation D and Regulation A+ are two common exemptions. These exemptions are subject to specific requirements, including restrictions on advertising or solicitation and limitations on the number and type of investors.

When pitching potential investors, StartUps must also take care of. For example, securities laws limit the information that investors can share. They also require that any information given to them is accurate and does not contain misleading information. In addition, financial projections must be supported by data and based on reasonable assumptions.

StartUps should be aware of ongoing reporting and disclosure obligations as part of raising capital. To ensure compliance with securities laws, StartUps must navigate the legal landscape carefully when raising capital. Working closely with legal counsel will help StartUps understand the limitations and requirements of each exemption and ensure compliance during the fundraising process.

A successful StartUp requires that you navigate the legal landscape. StartUps must understand the legal issues and take steps to minimize risks and comply with regulations. This process includes incorporating your StartUp, selecting the right legal structure and protecting your intellectual properties, negotiating contracts, and complying with regulations specific to your industry.

StartUps must also comply with securities laws when raising capital. To avoid legal issues, StartUps must understand the legal requirements for fundraising and plan their capital-raising strategies carefully.

StartUps can build a solid growth and success foundation by proactively addressing legal issues. Working with an experienced lawyer is crucial to ensure your StartUp is protected and fully compliant.

Chapter 31
Tailoring your Pitch for Specific Industries

One Size Does Not Fit All

StartUps often expand into new industries and sectors as they grow. This can present exciting opportunities and pose unique challenges, especially when pitching to investors and potential customers. In addition, every industry has unique nuances and needs. Therefore, a one-size fits all approach to pitching will not be effective.

This chapter explores the importance of tailoring a pitch to a specific industry or sector and guides how to pitch effectively to different verticals. We will explore several key industries, including healthcare, technology, finance, and financial services, as each presents unique challenges and opportunities. We will also provide tips and strategies to research and understand different industries so your pitch resonates and your StartUp is positioned for success.

Understanding the Unique Characteristics of Different Industries and How They Affect the Pitching Process:

Understanding each industry's unique characteristics is important to develop an effective pitching strategy. Investors evaluate StartUps based on each industry's challenges, trends, and opportunities. The healthcare industry, for example, is highly regulated and requires extensive regulatory approvals and clinical testing. Meanwhile, the software industry is characterized by rapid innovation and iteration. Therefore, understanding the specifics of your industry is key to creating a pitch that will resonate with investors.

Understanding the industry's landscape and identifying the major players in each vertical is important. For example, it's important to know the roles of wholesalers and retailers in the retail sector as they play an integral part in the supply chains. In addition, you can tailor your pitch by knowing who the decision makers are, their challenges, and their priorities. Understanding the industry, its stakeholders, and your target audience will help you craft a pitch that speaks directly to their needs and shows that you can navigate the industry's landscape.

Researching the Industry and Identifying Key Players, Trends, and Challenges:

To tailor your pitch for a particular vertical, it is important to research and identify the industry's key players, challenges, and trends. Understanding the market, the competition and the trends will make your pitch craft a pitch more targeted and address the needs and pain points of your audience.

Begin by doing market research to identify major players and trends within the industry. Next, you can analyse industry publications, online forums, or news articles. Finally, you can use your network to reach industry experts and gain insights into market dynamics and pain points.

Identify the challenges and pain points your audience faces. These issues may be related to supply chain management or customer acquisition. You can show that you understand the industry by addressing these issues in your pitch.

Consider the competitive environment and how your product stands out in the market. You can highlight your unique business model, technology, or value proposition. You can show your market success and share by differentiating yourself from your competitors.

You must research and identify key industry players, trends, and challenges to create a pitch that will resonate with your audience and gain their investment.

Analysing and Researching the Industry to Identify Trends, Pains, and Innovation Opportunities:

You must first research and analyse the industry to tailor your pitch for a particular vertical. Understanding the current industry landscape, identifying trends and pain points, and pinpointing the areas where your StartUp can make a significant difference is essential. This research will help you create a pitch that addresses the needs of the industry and shows how your StartUp can provide a unique proposition.

Start your research by identifying reliable sources of industry information. These sources may include industry associations, trade publications, market research reports, and government agencies. These sources can provide information on market size, growth rates, and emerging trends.

Then, perform a competitive analysis to better understand key players and their positioning in the market. This will help you identify the market gaps and how your StartUp can fill them. It can also help you differentiate your product from your competitors.

Researching the challenges and pain points of the industry is also essential. You can do this by talking to experts in the industry, attending events, and networking with professionals. You can use these pain points to tailor your pitch and show how your StartUp can provide value for the industry.

Identify areas where you can innovate and disrupt the industry. For example, identifying new technologies or business models that will revolutionize an industry or finding new solutions to existing problems may be necessary.

To tailor your pitch for a particular vertical, it is important to research and analyse the industry. Then, you can create a pitch by understanding the industry, its pain points, and opportunities. This will help you to develop a pitch that speaks directly to their concerns and shows the unique value that your StartUp can offer.

Develop a Value Proposition Aligned with Industry Needs and Priorities:

A successful pitch requires a value proposition aligned with the industry's needs and priorities. First, entrepreneurs must thoroughly research the industry to identify pain points and innovation opportunities. Then, they should develop a clear idea of how their service or product can solve these problems or take advantage of these opportunities.

It should highlight the product or service's advantages to the industry, for example, increased efficiency, cost-savings, better customer service, or improved performance. The value proposition should also address any objections or concerns the industry might have, including data privacy, regulatory compliance, or integration with the existing system.

Entrepreneurs should also tailor their value proposition according to the needs and priorities specific to each industry.

For example, the healthcare sector could focus on improving patient outcomes while reducing costs. On the other hand, the finance industry focuses on reducing fraudulent activity and improving security.

Developing a value proposition aligned with the industry's needs and priorities will demonstrate the worth of the product or services and convince investors or partners to become involved.

Use Case Studies or Success Stories to Establish Credibility with Investors and Customers:

Case studies and success stories from your target industry are a great way to gain credibility and trust among potential investors and customers. In addition, you can build trust by demonstrating your Startup's track record in solving similar problems and achieving similar goals.

To effectively use case studies and success stories in a pitch, you must first identify and research relevant examples within the industry. You can do this by looking at news articles, reports on the industry, or competitors to identify companies and individuals that have had success in similar areas. After you have identified examples of similar companies or individuals, you can craft your pitch so that you highlight how your StartUp could achieve similar results.

You must be transparent when presenting success stories and case studies. However, it can build trust among potential investors and customers by showing that you understand the industry and aren't making unrealistic claims or exaggerating capabilities. You can also highlight your Startup's unique insights and innovations. This can help differentiate your solution from other solutions and build credibility.

Adapt Your Pitch Style and Language According to the Culture and Norms of the Industry:

Successful pitching requires you to adapt your style and language according to the culture and norms of the industry. The communication style, culture, and values of different industries can significantly impact how investors or customers view your pitch. For example, a pitch for a tech StartUp might be more effective by focusing on technical details and innovation. However, a pitch to a healthcare StartUp must emphasize patient outcomes and regulatory compliance.

Research is essential to understand the culture of the industry and its communication style, including jargon usage, tone, and formality. You can then tailor your pitch according to your industry's preferences, increasing your chances of connecting with your audience. It would help if you also thought about the audience you would pitch to. This could include individual investors, venture-capital firms, or potential clients. It would help to consider that each group would have different communication expectations and preferences.

You can build trust and rapport with your audience by adapting your language and pitch style. The right language and tone can help you to appear more credible and knowledgeable in the eyes of your audience. This will increase their trust in your ability to deliver on your promises. It is important to find a balance when tailoring your pitch for the culture of your industry while maintaining your authenticity.

Include relevant data, metrics, and case studies to demonstrate the potential impact of your StartUp in the industry.

It's important to support your claims when pitching to investors or clients in a particular industry with data and metrics. Therefore, conducting thorough research into the industry is important to identify key performance indicators (KPIs), benchmarks, and other metrics used by investors or customers to evaluate possible investments or partnerships.

Understanding these KPIs will help you tailor your pitch to emphasize how your StartUp can assist investors or customers in achieving their goals and improving their bottom line. You can do this by presenting case studies and success stories of other companies that have achieved similar outcomes to yours and using data and metrics.

Consider how industry-specific challenges and pain points may impact your presentation of data and metrics. For example, if the industry is highly-regulated or risk-averse, you may have to demonstrate how your solution can mitigate specific risks or conform to relevant regulations.

When tailoring your pitch for a particular industry, including relevant data, metrics, and case studies is important. You can use this to help customers or investors see the value of your solution, and you can build trust and credibility with key stakeholders.

Addressing Concerns and Objections Specific to the Industry in the Pitching Process:

It's crucial to anticipate any objections or concerns that potential customers or investors may have. You must have a thorough understanding of your business and its challenges. For example, investors in the healthcare sector may be concerned about regulatory compliance or the time required to get FDA approval. By addressing these concerns in advance, you can build credibility and trust.

Researching the industry and its pain points and challenges is crucial to address concerns and objections effectively. Gathering data and case studies demonstrating the Startup's capability to overcome these challenges may be necessary. You should also be open and honest about any risks or limitations. Then, have a plan to address them.

To address industry-specific objections and concerns, it is

important to demonstrate a thorough understanding of the ecosystem of that industry. This includes key players and competition. In addition, it can demonstrate that you are realistic about the industry and where your StartUp might fit.

Remember that different industries will have different objections and concerns. For example, investors in the food and drink industry may be concerned about your product's scalability or the competitive landscape if you pitch them. By addressing these concerns in an industry-specific way, you can build investor confidence in the ability of your StartUp to succeed.

Case Studies and Examples of Successful Pitches Across Industries:

Entrepreneurs who want to customize their pitches for specific verticals can benefit from case studies and examples of pitching success in other industries. StartUp founders can learn from these examples about the specific characteristics of each industry, the needs and preferences of investors and customers, and the strategies and techniques used to secure funding and partnerships.

Colour Genomics is a good example of how to make a pitch that works in the healthcare sector. The company offers genetic testing for cancer risk and heart disease. Colour Genomics' pitch highlighted the importance of genomics for personalized medicine and how their technology could save lives and lower healthcare costs. Colour Genomics also highlighted its experienced team of healthcare and technology experts and their partnerships and leading healthcare institutions.

Zipline, a StartUp in the logistics and transport industry, has also made a pitch. Zip line provides drone-based services to deliver medical supplies and vaccinations in difficult-to-reach locations. Zipline's pitch highlighted the urgent requirement for more reliable and efficient healthcare logistics in developing nations and the potential of their technology to revolutionize healthcare supply chains. Zipline also highlighted their successful pilot projects in Rwanda and Ghana and their partnerships between government agencies and healthcare organisations.

Kiwi Campus, a food and beverage StartUp, is a third example. Kiwi Campus provides autonomous robots to deliver food on college campuses. Kiwi Campus' pitch highlighted the increasing demand for sustainable and convenient food delivery options by college students and the potential of their technology to disrupt traditional food service. They also highlighted the innovative robot design and their successful pilot program on multiple college campuses.

ZocDoc is an online platform that connects doctors and patients. The company's pitch focused on easing patients' pain when booking doctor appointments. It highlighted that their platform makes it easier to manage and schedule appointments. In addition, ZocDoc provided statistics on how many people struggled with the same issue and showed that their platform has already helped millions.

Coursera is an online platform for education that has successfully demonstrated its value proposition. It did this by showing how it addresses the challenges in traditional education. They emphasized how their platform makes education more affordable and accessible, allowing people to learn at their pace. Coursera provided statistics on how many people had already benefited, including millions from all over the world.

Opendoor is an online platform for real estate. It emphasized the inefficiencies of traditional real estate transactions and their pain points. They showed how their platform made it easier for people to sell and buy homes. Opendoor provided information on how many homes it had sold and the positive feedback it received from customers.

Transfer Wise is a financial technology firm that pitched its innovative solution for traditional money transfers' high fees and hidden costs. They discussed how their platform was a transparent, cost-effective, and efficient method for sending money to people around the globe. Transfer Wise provided statistics on how many people had used the platform and how much money they'd saved.

One Acre Fund (which provides financial and technical support to smallholders in Africa), successfully presented its value proposition by highlighting the difficulties of farming in this region. They showed how their platform gave farmers access to funding, training, and support, which helped them increase their yields and improve their lives. In addition, one Acre Fund provided data about the number of farmers that they have already helped and their impact on them.

These examples show the importance of understanding unique characteristics in different industries. They also demonstrate adapting pitch style and language according to industry norms and culture. StartUps can improve their chances of pitching to customers or investors in different industries by incorporating data, metrics, and case studies and addressing specific industry concerns and objections.

Understanding different industries' key players, trends, and challenges is essential to a successful pitch. To create a pitch that resonates, it is important to conduct thorough research, analyse data, identify pain points, and identify opportunities for innovation.

Success in pitching depends on adapting the pitch style and language according to the industry culture, including relevant metrics and case studies, and addressing objections and concerns specific to the industry.

StartUps can gain credibility and trust from potential investors and customers by incorporating case studies, success stories, and a value proposition aligned with the needs and priorities of the industry.

Case studies and examples of pitching strategies that have been successful in other industries can also provide StartUps with valuable insight and inspiration. By tailoring their pitches to the needs and characteristics specific to their target industry, StartUps will increase their chances of getting funding or gaining traction.

Chapter 32
The Future of Investor Pitching

Trends and Innovations to Watch

The landscape of investor pitches has changed dramatically in recent years. More innovative and streamlined methods have replaced in-person meetings, lengthy slideshows, and other traditional approaches to pitching. It is vital that entrepreneurs stay abreast of the latest trends in investor pitches as technology advances and the StartUp ecosystem evolves.

This chapter will discuss the future of investor pitches, trends, and innovations entrepreneurs should know. We will explore how new technologies like artificial intelligence, block chain, and virtual reality are changing the pitching process. We will also examine the increasing importance of sustainability and social impact in StartUp pitches. We will also discuss the rise of new platforms and investment models, including crowd funding and impact investments, and how they have changed how StartUps raise money. Understanding these trends and innovations will help entrepreneurs stay on top of the game and ensure their pitches in an ever-changing StartUp ecosystem are engaging and effective.

Use AI and Machine Learning to Improve Pitching:

In an age of rapid technological advancement, StartUps must stay abreast of the latest trends in investor pitches. Latest developments like Artificial intelligence (AI), machine learning (ML), and other emerging technologies are becoming increasingly popular in investor pitching. These emerging technologies can help StartUps improve their presentations, increase their chances for success and gain a competitive advantage in the market.

AI and ML are useful in many ways to improve the pitching process. For example, StartUps can use AI-powered tools to analyse data. They will be able to identify trends and patterns within their target market. The information obtained can be used to create more effective and targeted pitches that will resonate with investors. The ML algorithms also analyse previous pitching performances and identify improvement areas.

Chatbots and virtual assistants are another way StartUps can use AI and ML to pitch. These tools automate certain parts of the pitching procedure, like answering common questions or providing additional information on the StartUp. As a result, it saves both the investor and the StartUp time and ensures they receive accurate and consistent information.

AI and ML can help StartUps stand out and improve their chances of success in a crowded marketplace. However, StartUps must approach these technologies cautiously, as they are still in the early stages. Therefore, working with professionals who are experienced in these technologies is essential. They can guide their implementation and ensure they are used ethically and effectively.

Virtual pitching: Best Practices to Engage with Investors and Present Remotely:

Virtual pitches have become more common recently, especially in light of the COVID-19 pandemic. As remote work and virtual events become more common, StartUps must adapt their pitching strategies to engage potential investors online.

For StartUps to make the most out of virtual pitches, they should create an engaging and compelling presentation. This will capture investors' attention while communicating their value proposition. Using high-quality audio-visual equipment and including interactive elements such as polls, Q&As, and demos is important.

Virtual pitching also requires mastering virtual communication. It is important to build rapport with investors via video conferencing. StartUps must also adapt their presentation for the virtual environment. This includes adjusting content and pacing to keep investors focused and engaged.

Virtual pitching allows StartUps to reach a wider range of investors regardless of their location or time zone. By using virtual platforms, StartUps can participate in global pitches and connect with investors around the globe, expanding their network.

StartUps increasingly rely on virtual pitching to grow businesses and connect with investors. StartUps can use the new trend by following the best virtual communication and presentation practices.

The Rise of Video Pitches - Tips on Creating Compelling Video Pitches:

Video pitches have gained significant momentum over the past few years as investors increasingly prefer to view pitches remotely. Video pitches can be a powerful way to attract investors' attention and communicate your message engagingly and clearly. It is important to tailor your video pitch according to the specific characteristics of the medium.

Video pitches offer the opportunity to make your pitch come alive with visual aids, storytelling techniques, and customer testimonials. It can be anything from graphics and animations to customer testimonials and live-action footage. Use these elements to build a compelling story that explains the product or service and creates excitement and emotional engagement.

Notably, the quality of production and the technical aspects are equally important in creating a successful video. It is important to pay attention to lighting, editing, sound quality, and the platform and distribution format. Many tools and platforms are available to help StartUps create high-quality video presentations with little technical knowledge.

When creating a video presentation, it is important to balance brevity and substance. Keeping your video short and sweet is crucial but provides enough information to get investors' attention. Investors receive a lot of pitches. This balance can be achieved with a well-crafted script, which includes a clear value proposition, a summary of your team's experience, and a description of your market opportunity.

Many StartUps use video in other ways than just as a pitching tool. Some companies, for example, have used video to complement their written pitch decks, adding context and explanations of key points. In addition, some companies have used video to follow up on in-person or online pitches. This allows them to reinforce their messages and keep investors interested.

Video pitches reflect a trend toward more innovative and dynamic approaches to investor pitching. By leveraging this unique medium, StartUps can create more engaging and memorable presentations. This will help them stand out in a crowded market.

Investor Preferences - What StartUps can do to Keep up With the Trends and Stay Ahead:

Investor preferences continue to change as the StartUp scene evolves. To stay on top of the game, StartUps must understand how investor preferences change and adjust their pitching strategy accordingly. For example, investors are increasingly looking for StartUps that prioritize social and environmental responsibility alongside financial return. This is one trend that has emerged over the past few years.

In addition, diversity and inclusion are becoming increasingly important in the investment process. Investors are increasingly investing in StartUps led by women and people of colour. They also invest in other underrepresented groups.

The pandemic also has caused a shift in the way investors conduct due diligence online and make investment decisions. As a result, StartUps must be ready to adapt to the new reality and have strong virtual pitching abilities.

Investors are increasingly interested in StartUps that use emerging technologies like AI and Block chain to drive innovation and disrupt established industries. In addition, investors will be interested in StartUps that incorporate these technologies effectively into their pitching strategy.

In today's fast-paced StartUp world, staying abreast of trends and investor preferences is essential to a successful pitch. In addition, understanding and incorporating trends into pitching strategies can help StartUps increase their chances of securing the funding needed to grow and flourish.

Collaborative Pitching:

How StartUps can work with other companies to leverage their network and improve their pitch. In a new trend, StartUps are collaborating with other organizations or companies to develop a compelling and comprehensive pitch. By leveraging the combined resources, networks, and expertise of StartUps, they can increase their visibility, credibility, and chances of success.

A great way to collaborate with other StartUps is to join forces in the same industry or vertical. By pooling their resources and presenting together, StartUps can create an impressive pitch highlighting each company's strengths and synergies. This can help StartUps to share costs and the workload of pitching. It will also make it easier for them to attend more events and reach out to more investors.

Partnering with well-established companies, organizations, or individuals within the industry is another way to collaborate. In partnering with an established partner, StartUps can leverage their expertise and credibility to gain the confidence of potential investors. This can give StartUps access to new markets, resources, and networks that will help them scale and grow their business.

Customers, users, or communities can be involved in the pitching process by StartUps. StartUps can make their pitch more compelling and customer-centric by incorporating testimonials and feedback from their target audience. This can help StartUps create a loyal customer base, which can be a valuable asset in the future.

Collaboration in pitching is a powerful way for StartUps to stand out in a competitive and crowded market. Working together and leveraging networks and resources can help StartUps create a convincing pitch that will resonate with investors.

Personalization - How StartUps can Customize Their Pitch to Investors:

The ability to personalize your pitch is crucial to a successful pitch. It allows StartUps to cater their pitch to meet each investor's needs, preferences, and interests. In addition, customizing their pitch will enable StartUps to demonstrate a greater understanding of an investor's investment history, expertise in the industry, and goals. This can increase trust.

Start by researching the investor's background, investment history, and areas of interest. You can then tailor your pitch to address the pain points, opportunities, and challenges that the investor is most interested in. In addition, this information can be used to show how your Startup's value proposition addresses the specific needs or issues and how your team's expertise and experience align with the investor's industry focus.

You can also personalize your pitch by leveraging your network and existing relationships. StartUps can learn valuable information about the investor by collaborating with industry experts, mentors, or advisors in a relationship with them. They can then tailor their pitch to match the investor's tastes better. These relationships can also be used to get warm introductions from the investor. This can increase the likelihood of getting funding.

Personalization is key to a successful pitch because it allows StartUps to show that they understand the investor's needs and goals, increase trust and increase their chances of getting funding. In addition, research, industry knowledge, and relationships can be used to tailor a pitch for each investor. This will help them stand out from the crowd.

Social Impact Pitching:

Social impact pitching is pitching investors interested in investing in companies with positive social and environmental impact and financial returns. StartUps must demonstrate their financial potential and commitment to making a positive social and environmental impact.

A good way to communicate the Startup's social and environmental impact is by clearly communicating the product or service. This could include metrics like carbon emissions reduction, waste reductions, or social outcomes such as job creation, community empowerment, or improved access to education and healthcare, agriculture and irrigation, protection of forests etc.

A second important consideration is that the company's values and mission should align with the impact investor. StartUps can identify impact investors with a track record of investing in similar companies and values and tailor their pitch to them.

StartUps should also be prepared to discuss any social or environmental risks that may arise from their business model and how they intend to mitigate them. Impact investors will often be highly focused on ESG issues (environmental, social, and governance). They want to ensure that the company is in line with their values and meets their criteria.

StartUps can collaborate with social impact organizations and initiatives to strengthen their story of impact. For example, it could be partnering with other StartUps, non-profits, or industry associations to build a stronger social change ecosystem.

Pitching to Investors in Emerging Markets:

What StartUps need to know about pitching investors in emerging markets? Emerging markets are also called developing markets. They are economies that are in transition and are experiencing rapid development. These markets have high growth potential, low entry barriers, and a growing demand for new products. As a result, StartUps are increasingly turning to emerging markets for investment and growth.

Pitching investors in emerging markets is different from pitching investors in developed markets. This subtopic will cover the best practices to follow when pitching in emerging markets and what StartUps need to know before they pitch investors in this region.

1. **Understanding the Market:** StartUps must understand their target market before they can pitch to investors. Understanding the country's culture, language, and business practices, as well as the legal and regulatory framework, is essential. StartUps should also be aware of the challenges and opportunities that the market presents, including the lack of capital and infrastructure and the potential for rapid growth.

2. **Create Local Partnerships:** Success in emerging markets is largely dependent on building local partnerships. Local partners with a strong understanding of the local market can offer valuable insights and connections. In addition, local partners can assist StartUps in navigating the local business climate and building relationships with investors.

3. **Value Proposition Communication:** StartUps must be able to clearly explain their value proposition and how this aligns with local needs and priorities when pitching investors in emerging markets. StartUps should also be ready to discuss how they plan to address any challenges or opportunities that may arise

in the local market.

4. **Be Flexible:** StartUps must be flexible to adapt and change to emerging markets' rapidly changing and uncertain nature. Therefore, StartUps need to be ready to adapt their business strategies or models in response to market conditions and investor feedback changes.

5. **Build Trust:** In emerging markets where investors are wary about investing in StartUps that are new or have not proven themselves, building trust is essential. Therefore, StartUps must build relationships and show commitment to the market and the local community. It can be as simple as partnering with local groups or launching social impact initiatives.

Pitching investors in emerging markets can be difficult, but they also offer tremendous opportunities for innovation and growth. StartUps can improve their chances of succeeding in these rapidly changing markets by understanding the market, forming local partnerships, communicating value propositions, being flexible and building trust.

Non-traditional Pitches:

Non-traditional pitches have become popular in recent years to impress investors quickly and easily. The elevator pitch is one such method. During an elevator ride or other brief encounters, a founder only has 30 seconds to 2 minutes to present their idea to investors.

Speed dating is another non-traditional format of pitching. StartUps rotate through quick pitches with different investors over a short period. This format allows StartUps to pitch multiple investors at a single event and get feedback from different perspectives.

Pitch competitions and hackathons are other non-traditional methods of pitching. These allow StartUps to present their ideas to a large group of investors, mentors, and partners.

Non-traditional pitches can be innovative and exciting but require a different strategy and approach than traditional formats. StartUps need to be able to distil their message and value proposition in a concise, impactful pitch that can grab the investors' attention. In addition, the pitch must be adaptable to different formats, time constraints and still communicate the main points of your business.

It's also important that StartUps stand out and distinguish themselves from their competition. A unique and memorable pitch can help achieve this, as well as a clearly defined value proposition and an engaging story.

StartUps can benefit from non-traditional methods of pitching to get exposure, improve their pitch, and connect with investors. Understanding the unique challenges of these formats will help StartUps maximize their chances for success and make them stand out amongst a crowd of competitors.

Investor pitching is changing rapidly. New technologies and trends influence how StartUps present their ideas and raise money. The StartUps that adopt these innovative pitching methods and stay on top of the latest trends will have a better chance to stand out and attract investors in a crowded marketplace. StartUps can improve their chances of success by incorporating AI, machine learning, virtual and video pitches, personalizing pitching, and considering non-traditional formats. StartUps can also adapt their pitching styles to suit different industries, investor tastes, and emerging markets.

Chapter 34
Conclusion

Pitch Like A Pro: Decoding Investor Pitch is a comprehensive book that gives entrepreneurs and StartUps all they need to know about creating a winning pitch and securing funding. The book has covered many topics, including understanding the investor's mind-set, creating a compelling value proposition, preparing a presentation, and delivering a confident pitch.

We have stressed the importance of research, preparation, and communication during pitching. To increase your chance of success, we have highlighted the importance of tailoring your pitch for specific industries, audiences, and investors. This final chapter will review the main lessons from the book and show how they can be put into practice.

Lessons Learned:

1. Understand the investor's mind-set. Investors want StartUps with a clear value proposition, a strong market opportunity, and a team of professionals who can

execute the plan. Before you begin crafting your pitch, it is important to understand what investors are looking for and their perspectives.

2. Create a compelling value proposition. Your value proposition must clearly explain how your StartUp solves problems, what benefits it offers, and why you are different from other solutions on the market. Focus on customer benefits and use data to back up your claims.

3. Prepare a powerful pitch deck. Your pitch deck must be clear, concise, and visually appealing. It should include all the important information about your company, such as your team, market, products or services, and business model. Keep it simple and easy to understand, and use data and graphics to back up your claims.

4. It is important to practice your delivery. How you present your pitch can be just as crucial as its content. Focus on your body language and tone as you practice your delivery. Engage investors and be confident.

5. Research your target audience and tailor your pitch to their needs and interests. Your pitch should be tailored to your target audience's specific needs and concerns. Use relevant metrics, data, case studies, and other information to show your industry knowledge.

6. You can enhance your pitch by using emerging technologies: AI, machine learning, video pitches, and virtual pitching tool are all ways to create a more effective and engaging pitch. Try these tools and techniques to see which ones work best for you and your StartUp.

7. Personalize your pitch. Investors will be more inclined to invest in StartUps with which they have a personal relationship. Research your potential investors, and customize your pitch according to their backgrounds,

interests, and personalities.

8. Be socially responsible. Investors are more interested in StartUps with a positive impact on society. Your Startup's impact on society should be communicated to investors.

Putting the Lessons into Practice:

Start by researching your audience, industry, and investors. Then, create a compelling value proposition and a visually appealing pitch deck highlighting your Startup's benefits. Finally, use case studies and relevant data to tailor your pitch and show your industry knowledge.

Try new technologies like AI, machine learning, video pitches, and virtual pitching to engage your audience and enhance your pitch. Your pitch should be tailored to the potential investor and highlight your Startup's social impact.

Remember that perfecting your pitch takes time and practice. Do not be afraid to ask for expert and investor feedback and refine your pitch.

Last Thoughts:

Pitching to investors is an important part of the StartUp journey. A successful pitch could mean the difference between getting funding and struggling to get an idea off the floor. We have discussed the essential elements of a successful pitch throughout this book. We cover everything from crafting a compelling pitch to understanding your audience to tailor your pitch for specific industries.

We also looked at emerging trends and innovations, such as virtual pitches and video presentations. The pitch process is changing, and StartUps must adapt to stay on top of the game.
The importance of developing strong relationships with

investors is the one thing that will always remain the same. The pitch is the first point of contact, but what happens after sets apart successful StartUps. You can convert a successful pitch into a long-term relationship by maintaining open communication and showing commitment to your idea.

Keep these lessons in mind as you continue your StartUp journey. First, passionately communicate your passion for your idea through a compelling story. Your pitch should be tailored to your audience. This could mean focusing on data and metrics or emphasizing the social impact of your concept.

Remember that a great pitch is just the beginning. It takes hard work and perseverance to build a successful business. You can turn your dream into a reality by staying focused on your goal and building a strong partnership with your investors.

We thank you for participating in this journey and wish you luck with your future pitches.

◆◆◆

What Next

Congratulations on successfully pitching your StartUp to investors and receiving funding! Now what? The pitch is only the first step on your StartUp journey, with much work still to be done to make your vision a profitable enterprise. In this chapter, we'll look at steps you should take to transform vision into reality and leverage investor relationships to expand and plan for your company's future.

Building a Strong Team Establishing the right team is paramount to StartUp success, and now is the time to assemble one. First, to execute your business plan effectively, identify key roles such as marketing, sales, and engineering needs. Once these have been identified, you should create job descriptions and start the hiring process; looking for candidates with experience and skills needed for implementation as well as culture fit is also a consideration; an ideal goal would be creating a team that functions smoothly while aligning itself around a common mission is desired.

Use Investor Relationships for Business Growth:

In addition to funding, investors may provide invaluable

resources and contacts that can aid your company in growing. Ask investors to introduce you to potential partners, customers, or advisors; investors may even provide industry knowledge or contacts that help overcome challenges or seize opportunities more effectively. Feel free to seek advice and support and update investors on progress or significant developments.

Scaling Your Business As your business expands, it is vital to prepare for scaling. Systems and processes need to be put in place to expand efficiently. Start by identifying which aspects of your company need to be scaled first - start by identifying those which need the most work on scaling first - make sure you have sufficient talent and resources available to implement plans effectively and consider investing in infrastructure or technology as needed to support expansion.

Plan for the Future Finally, it is critical that businesses plan for their futures. No matter its stage or stage of development, now is always the right time to consider long-term goals for your business - no matter whether that be five, ten, or twenty years down the line - what do your five-year, ten-year and twenty-year goals include in terms of growth, revenue and market share? Stay flexible and adaptable, as you must adapt quickly to changing business environments when setting these plans out.

Pitching your StartUp to investors is an essential component of the entrepreneurial journey. A comprehensive understanding of your company, market, target audience, and how they relate comes into play when crafting an engaging pitch presentation. Your pitch should only serve as the initial stage - to transform ideas into businesses. It requires a plan and implementation strategy, such as recruiting an effective team, cultivating investor relations, and planning long-term.

Entrepreneurship is not a sprint; it is a marathon. However, your vision can come to fruition with hard work and perseverance. Use this book's lessons to lay a solid foundation for your StartUp business while continuing your learning and expansion as an entrepreneur. We wish you success on your journey!

Author B M Aggarwal

The author would like to interact with you and would love to have your feedback.

You can get in touch with him and send your reviews.

Phone: +91 9650274066, 9599117721

Email: ipocare@gmail.com

LinkedIn: https://www.linkedin.com/in/bmaggarwal/

Facebook: https://www.facebook.com/CABMaggarwal/

Thank You

Afterward

Congratulations on finishing "Pitch Like A Pro: Decoding Investor Pitch"!

We hope this book has provided invaluable insights and practical strategies for creating an impressive presentation and securing funding to make your StartUp thrive.

As you consider the lessons from this book, it's essential to keep in mind that perfecting your pitch is a continuous process. While refining it, new challenges and opportunities will inevitably arise; with the right mind-set and approach, these obstacles can be overcome and fundraising goals achieved. Here are a few final points to keep in mind as you move forward:

1. **Keep Practicing:** Crafting an impactful pitch takes time and dedication - even for experienced entrepreneurs! Even newcomers should devote enough practice time to master pitch delivery until it becomes second nature. Record yourself so you can identify areas for improvement; seek feedback from peers, mentors, and investors on any potential improvements; seek feedback from the crowd at large about potential investors for advice.

2. **Stay Current:** The StartUp ecosystem constantly shifts

with emerging technologies, trends, and regulations altering the landscape. Stay informed by the latest industry news and trends that might impact your StartUp by subscribing to relevant newsletters, attending industry events, engaging thought leaders in your field, and subscribing to relevant newsletters - even subscribing to podcasts about StartUp success!

3. **Build Relationships:** Fundraising is about more than just raising capital; it should also involve forging long-term relationships with investors, mentors, and partners who will offer ongoing guidance to your StartUp. Be intentional in forging genuine connections with potential investors and stakeholders who may become long-term allies - show your gratitude by showing that you value their input while working collaboratively towards shared goals.

4. **Be Adaptable**: No two pitching situations are identical. Investors all have unique preferences, priorities, and decision-making processes that differ. Therefore, to meet each investor's needs with an effective pitch, you must adapt your pitch appropriately. Tailor your presentation specifically to each investor as necessary, be open to feedback from them, and be adaptable enough to pivot as required!

5. **Keep Your Eye on the Prize:** Your pitch's primary purpose should be securing funding to expand and scale your StartUp, so stay focused on this goal without being deterred by setbacks or rejection. Embark upon new paths enthusiastically, celebrate successes while learning from failures while always progressing towards your vision!

Other Book from the Author

Indian SMEs & The Power of SME IPO

Entrepreneurship has been a key part of the global economy since its inception. Small and medium enterprises (SMEs) are the backbone of any economy. These businesses are vital to economic growth, job creation, and innovation. However, SMEs have faced significant challenges in accessing finance, which has limited their growth potential and prevented them from reaching their full potential.

The introduction of SME IPO has significantly impacted the

lives of SMEs looking to access capital markets, unlock unmatched valuation & create unprecedented wealth. SME IPOs offer a way for SMEs to raise capital and expand their businesses by issuing shares to the public. This book provides valuable insight into the process, benefits, and challenges of going public for SMEs.

Being an entrepreneur, and consultant, I know first-hand the importance and necessity of capital access. This book has been written to be a practical and informative guide for SMEs who want to learn more about the IPO process. This book discusses various topics, including the benefits and disadvantages of going public and the requirements for an SME IPO. It also covers the legal and regulatory framework and the role of advisors, investment bankers and underwriters.

This book is likely to be a helpful tool for entrepreneurs who want to take their SMEs public and create unprecedented wealth. SME IPOs can transform the business landscape. I'm excited to share my experience and knowledge with other entrepreneurs.

This book also highlights a few success stories and impacts of going public for SMEs. These case studies offer valuable insight into the opportunities and challenges of going public, as well as the strategies that have been successful in helping SMEs navigate this process.

This book will inspire more SMEs to consider an SME IPO. It will also give them the information and knowledge they need to make informed financial decisions. SMEs have the potential to unlock untold wealth and increase their growth potential. This can help them contribute to the economic development of their countries and communities.

Thank you to all entrepreneurs who shared their knowledge and experiences with me while researching and writing this book. I also want to thank the experts who gave valuable advice and guidance.

Finally, I hope readers find the book valuable and informative in their quest to achieve their entrepreneurial goals.

To make the book more accessible, the author might have repeated phrases or paragraphs at specific places. This technique, also known as repetition, is used to reinforce key concepts and highlight key ideas. Repetition of certain words or paragraphs can help break down the monotonous complex information into smaller chunks that are easier to understand and retain. Repetition can also be a memory aid that allows the reader to recall important information.

The intentional repetition of phrases or paragraphs in this book can be a helpful tool for readers to understand better and retain the information.